WIPE

WIPE

Survival Tactics for Parents with Attitude

Penny Wilson

Hodder & Stoughton

First published in Great Britain in 2002 by Hodder and Stoughton
First published in paperback in 2003 by Hodder and Stoughton
A division of Hodder Headline

10 9 8 7 6 5 4 3 2 1

A CIP catalogue record for this title is
available from the British Library

ISBN 0 340 73355 1

Typeset in New Baskerville and Officina Sans by
Palimpsest Book Production Limited, Polmont, Stirlingshire
Printed and bound in Great Britain by
Mackays of Chatham plc, Chatham, Kent

Hodder and Stoughton
A division of Hodder Headline
338 Euston Road
London NW1 3BH

Contents

Welcome to Wipe

When I was younger, a lot younger, I absolutely knew that I was meant to have a large house, a gravel drive, 2.4 beautiful and healthy children and an obscenely rich and devastatingly handsome husband, along with unlimited access to cash. All topped off, perhaps, with just a little voluntary job to ease my social conscience.

Frankly, when the parenting hand was dealt, single parent, disabled child, housing association flat and constantly strapped for cash just wasn't quite what I'd envisaged. But there you go, life is rarely what you expect it to be. Especially where children are involved, as I've discovered.

And so it was that I found myself abandoning my former life as a social worker and bringing up an adorable but staggeringly strong-willed son. Not to mention spending more time with him in hospitals than seemed either right or fair, given that they bring both of us out in alarming rushes of intense stress. In between our hospital stays I would rifle optimistically through the parenting books and magazines in my local bookstore for something that would skip the 'how to do it perfectly' advice and stick to telling me the truth about bringing up a child. Just the painful, funny, sticky, exhausting truth.

Nothing doing. And so it was, one wintry evening, or was it one sunny morning – it's beyond my memory and its vastly reduced capacity to recall – that, armed with more children than sense, a girlfriend and I came up with the concept of *WIPE*. With blissful ignorance about the complex and problem-fraught business of producing a magazine, there was nothing to stop us going ahead. All we knew was that we'd had enough. No more parenting magazines that left us feeling inadequate or glossies that made us feel plain old. We wanted to produce something different. *WIPE – Parenting with Attitude* aimed to tell it how it really is rather than how we're told it should be, to bring parents together so they no longer felt alone with their age or inadequacies and to let parents laugh about just how tricky real-life parenting can be.

Against all odds we made it and *WIPE* was born in December 1999. Kind souls invested much more than faith, and while we had a ball publishing it, real parents got to write about real parenting in it.

Being approached to write *WIPE* the book was a different ball game altogether. Could we turn a successful magazine into a successful book? But never one to miss a challenge, a great deal older and not a lot wiser, with some insight into writing, editing and publishing, alongside the rollercoaster ride of parenting, I decided it had to be worth a go.

By this stage we'd closed the magazine which, fun though it was, had taken over our lives. And, as the book loomed on the horizon, my business partner was forced to admit that she now had so many children she had no time to write it, while I had so little sanity left that I agreed to do it. So with Jane plying me with caffeine and keeping me company through extensive episodes of writer's block, or perhaps just sheer sloth, we made it, and here it is.

So when you find yourself surrounded by useful, practical titles which leave you feeling inadequate and downright bored, reach for *WIPE*. It won't make your children happier, healthier or more politically correct, but you might just feel less isolated in the ensuing madness of parenthood. *WIPE* is by parents for parents, about being yourself, doing the best you can and, hopefully, laughing at our inevitable mistakes.

In the course of writing *WIPE* I spoke to many parents, single, double, triple and assorted flavours in between. Their contributions are what makes *WIPE* so unique. Many, many thanks to all of them for their honest, touching and enlightening stories.

There are many aspects to parenting that this book hasn't set out to look at. It doesn't begin to cover everything. Being all things to all people is never one of my better ideas. But for those areas it does cover, *WIPE* tells it how it is rather than how other people think it should be.

Perhaps a little cynical in parts, it was never designed to be cheesy. Life is already full of people dropping little one-liners backed up by excessive expressions of love. 'I could strangle him,' they confess. So why do they feel the need to back it up with a guilty and somewhat sheepish laugh promising us they wouldn't really? Did anyone out there honestly imagine they would? Just why are we so uncomfortable with confessing and expressing how we really feel from time to time when life has pushed us to the limit? So for all you sensitive souls, I apologise in advance for the relative lack of reassurance backing up many of the truths *WIPE* faces. Rest assured – I love my child.

WIPE isn't a book for earth mothers or the immaculate variety with more collagen and nannies than sense. *WIPE* is simply an irreverent survival guide for intelligent parents who retain the will to live. A book about the madness, the struggles, the demands, the challenges, the constant whirl round and round the proverbial mulberry bush, the real impact on you as a human being, on your sanity and your stress levels. And despite all that, just how rewarding and often ridiculously funny parenting can be.

It's life – just not as we knew it.

Why *WIPE*? Why not?

Flannel Panel

With eternal gratitude to Angus, Jane (we met and started a conversation that won't be over till we're dead), David, the Cbobb Clan and the Breakfast Club, not least Sheila and Nancy, for everything from caffeine to chocolate, encouragement and extreme tolerance along the way.

And to Caro, whose input, support and total lack of criticism has meant *WIPE* got published and I stayed relatively sane.

Thank you also to Crispin for inspiration, cooperation and the odd good word, to the *WIPE* shareholders, to Marc Berlin, and to every parent who faced, head-on, the best and worst of parenting for *WIPE*. Thank you also to Mike and Sophie for rock-like support, to Simon and my parents for both tolerance and childcare; to Bill W for saving my a***, and a debt of gratitude to Annie L, my Sponsette and MJB for sharing much sanity. And finally thanks to Bert and Ernie for keeping their eye on the ball and coming up with the most amazing match of all. Through Angus and Mr Prov my life became whole.

And to everyone else I have failed to name specifically, who will resent me for ever – thanks all the same.

1

In the Stirrups

Birth – there's no backing out now

From the moment we're required to pee in a somewhat unglamorous manner on a small plastic stick, our lives are unlikely ever to be the same again. Dignity, among other previously highly valued forms of self-respect, has begun to alter its form for ever.

Ever since I spied that thin blue line, perched on a loo generously provided by Network South West, in a small station somewhere south of civilisation (I couldn't wait until I got home, in case you wondered), I have been surprised, dazzled and amazed at the experiences that were to follow. Faced with an unplanned pregnancy I felt utterly calm and strong. Although the time and indeed the circumstances were far from ideal, I knew I was capable of raising a child and knew without a doubt that embryo and I were going ahead.

I have sometimes been disappointed with myself and the circumstances within which I made this life-changing discovery and decision, since I was in a relationship with a man with whom I had an uncertain future. I had, I suppose, always quite envied my happily married friends who I assumed lived my ultimate dream scenario in which to begin a family. However, with researching this book came the reassuring insider information that things aren't always as they appear.

> 'I had always expected I would be overjoyed. That I would fling myself passionately into the arms of my adoring husband upon which, like a movie character, he would present me with a large bunch of roses. But despite having planned the pregnancy, I cried. I knew a long and frightening voyage had begun. At five foot nothing was I big enough? Was I brave enough? Perhaps I was just too small and pathetic.'
>
> *Jane, thirty-six, mother of James, six*

> 'It was simply the best feeling ever. I was beside myself with excitement. In fact, I had a large drink and a cigarette to celebrate – after all I was approaching, or about to begin, a long period of abstinence.'
>
> *Sheila, thirty-four, mother of Lauren, six*

> 'When I found out my wife was pregnant I simply went numb. After the initial shock, I became very, very excited. I felt so proud. It definitely does something affirming to your maleness at some very deep archaic level. In some way I had done what I was supposed to do. I then developed severe neuroses and insisted we attend every available class within a vast radius of our home! I somehow knew it would be a valuable experience but in fact I can't remember a single thing they said. What

I do remember is of the six couples in the room, three of the other imminent fathers were my age so I felt less of a first-time, forty-something old freak. I also recall on one occasion they talked about how useful massage could be and when they asked for a volunteer to demonstrate on I stuck my hand up, only to be told it was for the women only. Somehow I'd imagined they'd deliver the baby with one hand and gently massage away my stress with the other.

'By the second week, I knew the news had had a very basic effect on me. When they asked how the week had been I had to confess that whilst the most amazing thing was about to happen to us I was convinced that something awful was wrong with me and that I wouldn't be around to experience it. It had begun to manifest itself in quite genuine physical symptoms and despite 100 per cent clear results from the brain scan and heart monitoring I had put myself through that week, it was only there that I had spoken about my fears of becoming a father for the first time. Apparently I had been having panic attacks.

'Finding out I was to be a dad brought everything to a head for me. It was about total, 100 per cent commitment. I felt as though a door had closed and it was very scary. This wasn't going to be an instantly gratifying experience, which is what I am naturally inclined to opt for. The benefits of parenthood are certainly medium, if not long term. But I made the right decision. My family has given a meaning to my life above and beyond all other aspects of it. They're everything.'

James, forty-nine, father of Maddie, five, and Mason, one

Battle plans and birthing partners

Having stopped reeling from the news and as the Armitage Shanks tattoo fades from our foreheads and the weeks of morning or, let's be honest here, twenty-four-hour sickness become transferred to our memory instead, it's onwards and outwards through the remaining months of pregnancy. Practical adjustments to be made, plots to be hatched, shopping to be done and, in between times, the perfect birth plan to be written, and birthing partner to be found. Then, having identified a suitable punch-bag, all we have to do is persuade them to come along for the ride.

I have to admit to harbouring, at that stage, a small romantic fantasy which I'm afraid to say resulted in a pain relief-free birth plan, incorporating a quick dip in the birthing pool if there was time, followed by the tearful moment of my rosy-cheeked, perfect child's arrival. My son and I held lovingly by the father, who was in turn overwhelmed with pride in his son and at my valiant bravery and non-complaining skills in the field of childbirth. Reality, however, was a drug-induced haze, culminating in a rather dramatic emergency caesarean section and, whoops, took my eye off the ball at some point, not a proud father in sight! My birth plan, upon reflection, was naïve to say the least, but apparently I'm not alone in that.

> 'I've written three now and each time I've got closer to achieving my aims. Perhaps experience has just made me a little more realistic as to what can happen during labour.'
>
> *Sophie, thirty-five, mother of Dan, seven, Joe, five, and Martha, two*

'I've got three children but only ever wrote a birth plan for the first. I was so far off sticking to it that I didn't bother again. After the pain and trauma of the first birth I knew I wasn't going to allow myself to go down that road again. So my other birth plans were just internalised ones that involved making sure the epidural happened almost immediately.'

Clare, thirty-nine, mother of Melissa, ten, Megan, seven, and Ben, four

And as for the birthing partners, surely most women choose the father – or do they?

'I always assumed that my husband would be my birthing partner – after all that's his job in the proceedings. When we discussed it, he swallowed hard and then agreed. I think if he'd insisted that he couldn't face it I would have been disappointed and then opted for a close friend who'd been through the experience so they would really understand.'

Rachel, twenty-five, mother of Zoe, two

'The father was there for all three of my births but I'm not sure that I ever really put much thought into who it should be. I think it just ended up being him because somehow that's who we think it ought to be. But I'm not sure they're necessarily the best person. On reflection I wish I had chosen a mate. Would I say my husband had been useful during the birth? Yes. But then I would say that anyone would be useful because all I needed was someone to blame for the pain I was in! If it ever happens again I'll definitely choose a

> friend because I might spend less time blaming them and more time getting constructive support.'
>
> *Janet, thirty-two, mother of Matthew, eight, Sam, six, and Jake, three*

Perhaps all we can conclude is that most of us automatically assume we want our partner to be there because in some way it's expected of them in today's society. And if it's your first labour it's very difficult to know what would be most helpful.

I particularly love the abundance of guidebooks offering advice like: choose a birthing partner who's closely involved during the pregnancy so they can provide you with emotional and physical support during labour – rubbing your back, mopping your brow, or holding you through a contraction. It all sounds so wonderfully calm and reassuring.

On reflection, I feel they undersold the option of verbal abuse, alongside murdering the man who got you into this mess in the first place.

Then there's the gem about getting your partner to ask questions on your behalf. I gave birth. I certainly didn't lose the power of speech.

On with the show

So nine months on – give or take a few days – it's time to play the waiting game. Most women, and indeed men, appear to spend these last few weeks fluctuating wildly between extreme relief the pregnancy is almost over, excitement at the imminent arrival and waves of anxiety. The good news is that constant visits to the loo are almost over, along with all the other discomforts that go hand in hand with the last days of pregnancy. But try not to be in too much of a hurry. New discomforts are lurking just around the corner. The best advice I got at this stage, and failed miserably to take, was rest as much as you can. Why rush? It'll come soon enough and once it does there's no turning back.

I filled my days swinging between strange nesting activities and experimenting with a variety of old wives' tales to try to speed up the process. In case you're tempted, and somewhat bored, you could always give them a go.

Don't pack your hospital bag, that's just asking for a delay. Then consume vast amounts of the hottest curry you can lay your hands on, drink obscene quantities of raspberry tea – you can't possibly go to the loo any more than you already do – then hop on to the bumpiest bus you can find. The number 24 was my particular favourite.

Other mothers I've spoken to had a much better time. Sex was their general recommendation. For pleasure I assume, but also because it stimulates the hormone that could trigger off contractions. Whichever old wife concocted that one had her head screwed on.

Having scared myself half to death with visions of how labour might start I have to say it was a somewhat disappointing and undramatic pessary insertion that finally induced my son into activity. However, this is certainly far from always the case. A 'show' – the plug of mucus that can appear at this stage – or the waters breaking, may herald the beginning of labour. Or you might just head straight into the contractions without any prior warning.

'I spent the vast majority of my last days of pregnancy browsing the aisles of M&S nurturing the vain hope that my waters would break and I would come into possession of a substantial number of gift vouchers that I thought they might distribute under such circumstances. Thank God it happened one day after I'd left because presenting me with a dinghy would've been more use. I could never have imagined what it was going to be like. It nearly took me off my feet!

'I arrived at the hospital and began to unpack my bag between contractions. I think my first real shock was when the midwife asked what all the magazines and books were for. I'd packed them thinking I was off for a stay in hospital for a few days. How naïve was I? I didn't flick through them then and five years down the line I still haven't. Contractions were unreal. Far, far worse than I could ever have imagined, which is probably a good thing or I would never have had a child at all.'

Delia, thirty-one, mother of Daisy, five

'The contractions weren't that bad, so I thought, but I have to confess when told this was just the beginning I insisted on an epidural for all three of my deliveries. Why be in pain when you don't have to? I really think they don't push that argument hard enough during your pregnancy. Midwives seem to have a nasty habit of saying, "You're nearly there – hang on," right in the middle of each contraction, when you yourself know that you've got more than a long way still to go. My advice is just insist on the epidural before it gets too bad.'

Marnie, thirty-six, mother of Jamie, eight, Sarah, five, and Rachel, two

'Contractions hurt like hell, and I do remember being grateful for the breaks in between. At least it's not like a relentless pain where there's no respite. And gas and air – I was completely stoned and happy throughout most of them and was very funny as a result, at least I thought I was. My husband and the staff looked unconvinced, but who was I to care!'

Laura, twenty-eight, mother of Mia, one

The midwife – a different breed

Childbirth specialists, qualified to take care of you for the duration of your pregnancy, the birth and beyond, midwives are a breed apart. Frighteningly efficient, competent and generally over-keen, the midwife's manner can prove anything from reassuring to somewhat disconcerting or simply irritating beyond belief.

Some women I spoke to couldn't praise their midwives enough, while others simply raised their eyes to the sky at the very mention of them.

'My second labour was managed by an enormous, extremely butch and hairy-faced male midwife, who could easily have been mistaken for a biker. But despite my initial reservations he was absolutely brilliant. He made me laugh, reassured me when I desperately needed it and managed my pain relief without question. He even overworked his shift to stay with us until our daughter was born. For the other two births I had a community midwife team who were again all excellent. Perhaps if I had gone into labour naturally they may not have been available at that time but I had problems with both pregnancies and had to be induced slightly early both times. On each occasion a midwife from the team who I knew came over and took us to the hospital and stayed until the children were born. I can't speak highly enough of them.'

Clare, thirty-nine, mother of Melissa, ten, Megan, seven, and Ben, four

Other women, however, including myself, describe being allocated a local team of midwives only to discover that having got to know them prior to labour, almost without exception they have been off duty, away on holiday or simply busy with another labour when you actually need them, leaving you in the capable hands of another, equally keen, but quite unknown professional on the hospital production line.

Perhaps the trick with midwives is never to assume they will be with you during your labour while also bearing the following points in mind.

- Never labour under the false belief that the midwife will hold your hand throughout the proceedings. Midwives have a quite extraordinary capacity for saying, 'Be back in a moment,' and disappearing for what seems like an eternity, generally just as you are hit by yet another tidal wave of contractual pain and agony. That is, of course, unless you go private – simply a more expensive form of torture that ensures their almost continual presence and keenness of spirit. Under such circumstances you have an abundance of midwives holding every available hand and an obstetrician too. The more the merrier.

- Get your head around the sudden loss of dignity you are about to undergo. The midwife, having finally reappeared, will soon be holding an apparently perfectly normal conversation with you while simultaneously familiarising herself with your records, all the time having a hand firmly lodged halfway up your insides. My personal experience was an assorted variety of medical staff all comparing the length of their fingers to see which one drew the shortest straw, so to speak, and got to reach my apparently unusually high cervix. 'Dr Longfingers' is unlikely ever to fade totally from my memory. Dignity really is a thing of the past.

- Finally, exhausted from giving birth, prepare to deal with their keen spirit once more. Questions such as 'Do you want to see the placenta?' just need a simple but firm reply. 'No' is usually all that is required. Why anyone should want to see her placenta, much less eat it, remains a total mystery to me.

A square peg from a round hole . . .

With so many possible ways of giving birth I presume that in an ideal world most, if not all, of us would choose a quick and relatively pain-free experience in the comfort of our own homes. But the one thing that's certain in the uncertain world of birthing is that things seldom turn out the way you planned . . .

'The actual birth probably ranks as one of the most amazing nights of my life. It happened at home and was, thankfully, very, very fast.

'We'd chosen a home birth because . . . actually, my wife chose the home birth. I didn't. It scared me and I was completely against it. Although I was reassured by our house being only two minutes away from the local hospital and once I had made certain they were fully aware of the situation and were on standby, just in case, it was easier to agree.

'My wife had been uncomfortable the previous night but insisted it wasn't the beginning of labour, so the next evening when her waters broke and the midwife arrived forty-five minutes later, by which time the baby's head was already out, it was all quite a surprise. It was the most magical experience. There was none of the mythological mess you hear about and the bedroom certainly didn't need redecorating. We cleared up and then had a cup of tea with the midwife who stayed for another couple of hours. Our eldest child never even stirred. We woke her later and she came in and chose her new, little brother's first clothes. Then we all got into bed together and fell into a deep, deep sleep. When I woke up with my head on the pillow staring at my family and our new baby, who had never even been out of our house, it couldn't have been better. Today I have to say that it has only ever been bettered by the arrival of our next son, also at home, and even faster than the last.'

James, thirty-nine, father of Maddie, seven, Mason, three, and Johnny, one

'Fantastic. Two births and both of them totally pain-free! My son took an hour to arrive and the worst bit about it was having to have my backside on display to the world. In the end I covered my head with a sheet because that way at least one end wasn't quite so exposed! My second took a little longer to deliver – two hours and I needed a little gas and air but really there was nothing to it. If the rest of being a parent weren't so difficult I'd have a child every day of the week, well every nine months anyway. I can only think that I'm some kind of human bus lane. The only downside about both pregnancies was the weight gain. Three stone with the first and two with the second and I still haven't lost any of it.'

Robin, twenty-nine, mother of Jenny, three, and Sophie, six months

'I just remember being overcome by a wave of total fear and horror. The obstetrician arrived with an item that resembled the ultimate in modern kitchen appliances which under normal circumstances I would have considered sticking down my sink, but apparently it was just another in the charmingly aesthetic range of instruments used to pull out stuck babies. My first birth had been a forceps delivery, so I wasn't having much more luck this time around. The ventouse one was less painful, slightly, but, oh yes, every bit as humiliating. And an episiotomy with both topped off the trauma nicely.'

Helen, thirty-one, mother of Laura, four, and Charlie, one

'"Gosh, that is a big one," the midwife declared nonchalantly as she stared at my first caesarean scar. Never a promising start. A second baby, a second form of torture and a second type of scar. The midwife arrived forty-five minutes after we did. We'd been stuck in a room on our own; I was eight centimetres dilated and experiencing hideously painful contractions. The only plus side had been the opportunity for the liberal and unsupervised use of gas and air. To this day I disagree with the midwife's decision to stop me using it. They seem quite happy to let you make nests in corners, even to let you eat your own placenta, so why won't they just let you get stoned?

'I can only describe this birth as medieval. Everything seemed to come out of every orifice. "Is there time for an epidural?" I asked pathetically. She responded by pushing the red emergency button and in flew the cast from *M*A*S*H*. No warning. No explanations. I could only assume I was about to die. "We must get this baby out now," muttered Hawkeye between my screams and Henry was delivered with a pair of barbecue tongs. "Gosh, that was an *ER* moment," laughed the bimbo in blue. I would definitely have hit her there and then, but my legs were in stirrups and stitching had begun. Walking was painful for four weeks. I was incredibly bruised and sore. I really believed it would be impossible ever to have sex again. How could I possibly forget so quickly and go on to find myself expecting a third? But you do forget, don't you? Eventually!'

Fiona, thirty-seven, mother of Poppy, six, Henry, four, and Hugo, two

'After a long and difficult labour my baby began showing signs of distress and after much painful fumbling as the contractions got closer, and the more intensely I screamed the doctors decided to give me a general anaesthetic. I was extremely angry that it took so much poking and prodding before they made this decision and that I then couldn't be awake for the birth. Once I was up and about again I realised I was still furious about the way I had been treated and I took the unusual step of returning to the hospital after I had fully recovered from the trauma to talk to the doctors involved. My complaint was that I had been made to feel like a piece of meat, that the doctor had seemed angry with me rather than sympathetic and that the violation and pain I had experienced had seemed unnecessary. The hospital apologised and I didn't take it any further. If there were ever a next time, I'd opt for an elective C-section, where I could prepare myself properly, suffer no hideous contractions or complications, no vaginal tearing and more importantly no trauma.

'On top of the traumatic birth I felt that having a C-section left me perceived as a failure. Real men don't eat quiche. Real women give birth vaginally.'

Sheila, thirty-four, mother of Lauren, six

'I think I must be one of the only women who's managed to have a child and a six-week check-up and still not have taken her pants off! When I was pregnant the gynaecologist only felt my stomach. Then followed a scan and an amnio which only required undoing my flies. Pants were firmly on again at the twenty-week scan and the consultant continued only ever to feel my bump as the weeks progressed. The closest we came was the elected caesarean section but even then a hospital pair stayed on. At the six-week postnatal check the doctor asked if I had stopped bleeding and when I said yes he announced I looked absolutely marvellous and that he wouldn't be bothering with an examination in that case. So, all that and pants off not once. No man, other than my husband, has been anywhere below my bikini line!

'In all seriousness, an elected C-section was the wisest decision I ever made. I spoke to so many people during pregnancy about what they would recommend and do understand that many people believe my decision was a cop-out. But I based it on a number of factors. Not least that, although not medically necessary, I felt at forty years old it would probably be safer to have my first child in a more controlled manner. Also, there are problems with a woman's body returning to normal following childbirth at any age, but at forty I'm certainly less elastic than your average twenty-two-year-old. On top of that, so many of the women I spoke to described natural childbirth as being a fairly traumatic experience. "A piece of meat on a slab" one girlfriend said and that wasn't an experience I particularly wanted to go through if it wasn't entirely necessary.

'I know that some people find operations frightening but to me an elected C-section made me feel more in control. My husband was fully supportive of the decision, as he wanted me to choose what made me feel safest and most comfortable about giving birth. And although many of my friends, particularly those who had C-sections themselves, said, "Well done. Brilliant," and were totally supportive, I was surprised at the depth of anger it brought up in some people. At the time I was quite upset but when I think about it now I'm not sure that the ones who got most upset weren't the ones who had to have loads of drugs during their own "natural" births. I'm a great believer in each to his or her own. It's just that the birthing-pool option isn't for me.

'In retrospect I'm so glad I made this decision. It was a hugely good and positive experience and I think my daughter and I are calmer and less traumatised as a result. Also she came out looking gorgeous and not even closely resembling a squashed prune – I just hope it lasts to her teenage years!

'I doubt we'll have any more children now but if we did I'd certainly make the same choice again. Without a doubt it was right for us.'

Rebecca, forty-two, mother of Claire, two

All this only leads me to conclude that there's no right or wrong way to give birth – just the best you can manage at the time. But one thing's for certain. Whether the experience is gruesome, plain sailing or simply somewhere in between, for the majority of us the minute we clap eyes on the end product, that bawling, red-faced little scrap of humanity, the agony fades into oblivion and a lifetime of besotted adoration begins.

Wipe wisdom

- Remove the word 'birth' and be a little more realistic. 'Battle plan' springs to mind.

- If you find you were a little too idealistic, don't give

yourself a hard time. After all you wouldn't have a tooth pulled out without pain relief. There's brave and then there's just plain foolish.

- Steer clear of opinionated women in capable skirts with an abundance of children.

- Steer clear, too, of cheerful creatures who want to share their horror stories. If they need therapy they can pay for it.

- Approach parenting as you would approach life. Strive to be honest and true, allow yourself to fail, learn from the mistakes and keep marching forward.

- If all else fails tell the doctors you are a lawyer based in New York. Get your husband to ask everybody their names and take notes.

Terminology:

What they say and what they really mean

After pains: and you thought it would be all over after the birth! Contractions which help your womb shrink back to normal size – not great, but to be expected.

Amniotic fluid: baby floats in this. Up to one and a half litres guaranteed to exit your body, probably at high speed, before birth.

Anterior position: baby lies with back of head facing the front of your pelvis. May turn around. Pain levels – approximately 8/10.

Anxiety: produces stress hormones such as adrenaline. You'll be told to relax and enjoy your pregnancy, as stress is 'bad for baby'. Sorry, darling.

Backache: oh, yes.

Braxton Hicks Contractions: may have them, may not. Contractions of the non-painful variety towards the end of your pregnancy – enjoy!

Breech baby: bottom down and no sign of turning. Generally results in an episiotomy or C-section.

Brow presentation: caesarean scar on its way.

Caesarean: operation to remove baby from the womb resulting in normal and perfect, uncomplicated sex life resuming in no time at all. Celebrate!

Cervical incompetence: a laughable term for a serious matter. Weakness of the muscles at the neck of the womb can lead to miscarriage, but don't despair, a stitch can be put in to keep the cervix closed.

Contractions: the excruciatingly relentless tightening of the womb's muscles. Enjoy the ever shortening respite between outbursts.

Due date: nine months and one week from the first day of your last menstrual period; figure that one out, Einstein.

Effleurage: not a word that can be taken seriously, along with the claim that this light massage of the tummy may be comforting during labour. Perhaps only to be relied upon in the early stages.

Enema: routinely used in the past before giving birth. Be grateful it's less common today!

Engorgement: feed the baby to reduce feeling hot, hard and extremely uncomfortable.

Entonox: 50 per cent oxygen and 50 per cent nitrous oxide for inhalation by mother. Great pain relief and entirely under your control. When in doubt get stoned – and it's legal.

Epidural: marvellous invention. Small injection in the spinal canal and for needle phobics, it's a physical impossibility to see them doing it. Pain following epidural 0/10.

Episiotomy: cross your legs now. Cut made through back wall of vagina to perineum to a) make enough room for the baby or b) to allow barbecue tongs to be placed around the baby's head.

Forceps: curved, stainless-steel barbecue tongs placed around baby's head. You push, doctor pulls.

Foremilk: thin and watery milk produced prior to arrival of hindmilk. Seems logical enough.

Haemorrhoids: grated raw potato placed on these varicose veins of the back passage are reputed to help! Alternatively, for the more conventional among you, doctors can give prescriptions for this sort of inconvenience.

Incontinence: do your pelvic floor exercises. Avoid sneezing and bouncy castles for quite some time.

Induction: labour started artificially by breaking your waters with a crochet hook, gels or pessaries to stimulate contractions when your child shows absolutely no interest in moving out.

Involution: when your womb shrinks back after childbirth. Does not guarantee your stomach, bottom and thighs will follow.

Lamaze method: involves learning detailed breathing patterns for coping with contractions. Instinct tells me Fernand Lamaze was a bloke.

Linea nigra: dark line appearing down middle of abdomen. Combined with a caesarean scar, greatly increases the likelihood of being mistaken for a hot cross bun.

Lithotomy position: stirrups to the layman. Lithotomy position to the pregnant woman the midwife doesn't want to alarm.

Lochia: the blood you lose for two to six weeks following birth.

Massage: rarely helps dramatically but indulge yourself none the less.

Mastitis: check with doctor if antibiotics are needed for breast infection, or if it's simply a blocked duct causing localised inflammation. Either one will hurt.

Meconium: try not to be alarmed if your baby's first bowel movement is black, sticky and closely resembling tar. Nappies can only get more pleasant – you'd think.

Montgomery's tubercles: nothing to worry about when you find these on your areolae. Due to general levels of discomfort at this time, apart from breast-feeding that's about all you will find there. Would be easier for all concerned if Montgomery could keep his tubercles to himself.

Nausea: who called it morning sickness? Relentless 24/7 vomiting is perfectly possible.

Obstetrician, NHS: specialist doctor available for complications and emergencies during childbirth.

Obstetrician, Private: specialist doctor available to hold your hand, difficulties or not.

Oedema: swollen ankles, toes and puffy fingers. Once GP has confirmed it's not pre-eclampsia, put your feet up and support tights on.

Oxytocin: along with syntocinon, these hormones help stimulate womb contractions. Two great reasons to have copious amounts of sex when your baby is overdue.

Pelvic floor exercises: do them however dull if you are to avoid public humiliation at a later date. See 'incontinence' to comprehend the necessity fully.

Perineum: where vaginal and anal muscles meet or where doctors perform episiotomies.

Pethidine: similar to morphine. Ten minutes to work.

Lasts two to three hours. Pros: effective. Cons: can make you and the baby nauseous and sleepy.

Pica: technical term for cravings. If used it may convince the layman that you're eating weird stuff like coal and mouldy flannels due to a legitimate medical necessity.

Placenta: baby's life-support system. Can be eaten. But why?

Presentations: not dissimilar to work. It's all about the angle the baby's decided to take and convincing everyone else they'll just have to go with it.

Prolapse: not just restricted to cows, unfortunately.

Show: pop along to the West End. It's more fun, entertaining and generally less painful, unless it's a bad production.

Stitches: something to look forward to. The good news is they dissolve, reducing the opportunity for future humiliation while having them removed.

Stretch marks: reddish streaks affecting breasts, thighs, abdomen and bum. Fading to pale silver in time. Massage, diet and vitamins may help, but didn't for anyone I know.

TENS: Transcutaneous Nerve Stimulation. Basically it involves electrocuting yourself to distract your attention from the pain of childbirth.

Trial of labour: it certainly is.

Vacuum extraction: ventouse. Looks a little, or in fact a lot like a sink plunger. Plunger on baby's head. Vacuum created. You push. Doctor pulls. Baby's pointy head will lessen with time.

Varicose veins: don't risk it. Put your feet up now.

Vernix: greasy coating on the baby. This must be what makes it slip out, oh, so easily.

Water birth: all very well if there are ten pools for you and the other nine women on the labour ward who've made the same choice. Check out likely availability to avoid disappointment.

2

Blood, Sweat, Tears and Two Hours' Sleep

The truth about the first few weeks

Despite what can easily seem like an eternity of excruciating pain and hideous procedures, thankfully for most women the agony of labour is miraculously and instantly erased once they're propped up in bed with their newborn infant in their arms, gazing adoringly into the crumpled little red face of Winston Churchill. Let's face it – it's a fact, nine out of ten closely resemble the great man for at least a month or two.

I remember the relief when, after nine long months of waiting and wondering I finally had my baby in my arms, my legs back down from the stirrups and my feet firmly on the ground. But recovering from the labour, the bruising, the C-section and the exhaustion was quite another story.

Whatever the circumstances of the birth, whether it's one of the relatively calm and collected minority, a planned epidural, a last-minute forceps job or a dramatic race to theatre for an emergency C-section, it takes time to recover, both physically and emotionally.

In many countries across the world it's accepted that

mother and baby need time to adjust, and there are rituals and traditions which support this. Women are encouraged to rest and bond with their babies while other family members produce all the food and take care of the household. Remind me to emigrate to one of these enlightened places if I ever have a momentary lapse and another child. Because in this so-called civilised society of ours we are apparently expected to leap up the minute we've given birth, get straight back to normal, cheery smile in place, baby propped under one arm and routines back in operation after a couple of days. Somewhere along the line we seem to have decided that because pregnancy and birth are natural processes, we're therefore not technically ill and have no right to complain, ask for help or lie around a minute longer than necessary.

I fell for this one hook, line and sinker and within hours of the birth I expected to get on with life pretty much as I had before, albeit with a small attachment. Ouch. It didn't take long to realise that this route was a mite unrealistic, and that while birthing techniques may have made tremendous advances in the last few thousand years our bodies haven't.

The body blues

Thought the birth was the worst part and that after a while everything would just pop back into place? Sorry, think again! Because the birth is just the beginning. There really is no justice. Having given birth it is apparently normal to carry on having contractions for several days afterwards. And these get even stronger after a second or third child. All you can do as you grit your teeth through them is hang on to the plus side: with each contraction the womb is returning to its normal size and that has to be a good thing.

About one in four of us has either an episiotomy, or a natural tear at some stage during the process. And swollen and sore just about sums up the post-episiotomy experience. 'Don't worry, I'll never be having sex again,' is the most frequent response to midwives offering contraceptive advice at this point. However the healing process is quite remarkable and normal sexual activity is likely to be resumed sooner than you think, even if things do feel a little different at first.

Then there's the after-bleeding, which in effect means having a very long and very trying period, relatively heavy for the first week and then lessening over the next five or so. Resist temptation to buy those last few plastic toys immediately prior to the birth and take out shares in a sanitary towel company instead. Less cute but far more beneficial in the long term.

'Despite the fact that I'm only five foot two, have large pear-shaped hips and mousy-brown hair I have always liked my body. Curvaceous, feminine and Rubenesque were adjectives I delighted in. My body was certainly no representation of twentieth-century beauty, but aesthetically I could handle that and so could my husband. My breasts were round and pert, my waist went in and my hips went out. Lying in hospital after my first child was born I knew things were going to be different. Catheter-tubed, caesarean-scarred, with a linea nigra running down my middle, I looked like an overweight hot cross bun. My body had changed completely and I didn't recognise it, or like it, any more. My breasts sagged and leaked milk. The entrance to my sexual core had a great big stonking scar running across the top of it and my once blooming stomach now flopped sadly over the top of my red, painful and wide scar.'

Laura, thirty-four, mother of Sam, three and Thomas, one

'Women love telling birth stories, but no one tells you about the bit after the birth, where you feel leaky, flabby and extremely tender just about all over. The post-birth contractions were ghastly; I yelled just as loudly as I had during the delivery. And I found the six weeks of bleeding a real chore; it's like a period which goes on and on and on. Was I glad when everything got back to normal. And it did, every time, which was a relief because there was a point after each birth when I wondered whether I'd sacrificed all hope of feeling normal again for the wailing infant who was keeping me awake most nights.'

Annie, thirty-eight, mother of Ben, fifteen, Tom, twelve, and Susie, eight

On top of all this your stomach will feel – and look – like a mass of pulpy, blubbery flesh without a hint of muscle or tone in it. Don't panic, in time it will diminish and, for the lucky ones, even get back to its old self. Personally, I have my figure back, it's just not the one I recognise from before. There's no point rushing headlong into a diet or exercise regime, post-birth just isn't the time for it. In the first place it won't work and in the second you need all your energy for coping with your baby. So forget willpower and settle for patience.

If you're really determined to work out then just begin with the pelvic floor. In fact even if you don't feel the need to exercise start those particular manoeuvres. If you ever want to sneeze or go on a bouncy castle with any degree of confidence and dignity again they're an absolute must!

Besides, child-rearing will provide you with endless opportunities to weight-lift, arm-wrestle, run up and down the stairs and push heavy weights. After a few months of carrying the child, pushing the buggy, mopping, cleaning, changing and staggering up and down all night you'll realise that you may never need to pay gym membership again. Now that's a bonus!

However, if you've had an episiotomy you may have to delay the pelvic floor exercises while you wait for it to heal. Carrying a rubber ring, piece of foam or pillow around with you to sit on for the first few days is also an absolute necessity. A friend of mine who refused to take the foam ended up sitting on one buttock for the entire length of a four-hour car journey. Not great.

'Oh the misery of it. I had a really deep episiotomy and I could hardly walk or sit for a week after the birth. It was excruciating and I was seriously scared that I'd never be able to wee again without shrieking in pain. As for the prospect of sex, I imagined that was out for life. A friend told me to put lavender oil in warm baths and that helped a lot. Plus the child's rubber ring my husband went out and got for me to sit on! After a week I began to feel human again and a month after the birth I could actually sit on a chair without wincing.'

Jo, thirty-nine, mother of Jake, three

'Having had two episiotomies and one natural tear I have to say that neither option was great. Healing-wise they were equally crap and I couldn't sit down or wee comfortably for weeks. Months even. The most comfortable place to be was in a lavender or sea salt bath which I wanted to be left in for ever. It was the only place where I hurt less and got left in peace. Getting out meant I had to dry myself off and that hurt like hell. The other trick I learned was not to wee unless in a sea salt bath. I know it sounds disgusting but it hurt so much less it was the only way I could bear it at first.'

Clare, thirty-seven, mother of Chloe, seven, James, five, and Hannah, two

Then there are your breasts. Following the production of colostrum for the first few days you can expect to have hot, hard, swollen and sore breasts once the milk comes in, at around day three.

I remember the midwife dismissively terming it 'engorgement' while I remained convinced of a hideous medical disorder developing under their noses. Fascinated and slightly horrified by these enormous apparitions, I finally stopped panicking enough to feed the baby. It helped!

Of course some women sail through the breast-feeding bit, don't get engorged and wonder what all the fuss is about. But I haven't met that many of them. For most of us it's the grisly business they don't tell you about in birthing classes in case the prospect of pain followed by more pain is just too much to face.

'The birth of my first baby went really well. I wanted a natural birth and went to active birth classes so that I'd know what positions to try and how to manage the pain without drugs. In the end it was very quick, which helped because the pain was worse than I'd imagined. I got through it without drugs and felt really proud of myself when it was all over. My baby girl was gorgeous and the two of us fell asleep for about eight hours. But oh, God, the shock of what happened to my breasts. No one had told me what to expect and I was in agony, it was honestly worse than the birth. My breasts were like enormous, rock-solid balloons, so hot you could have fried an egg on them. The midwife told me to massage them, so I knelt over the bath, weeping and massaging and dripping milk, but it didn't help. Then we tried the cold cabbage leaves – no good either. I kept trying to feed my baby, but my breasts were so hard that she couldn't latch on properly. So she was crying with hunger and I was crying with pain and frustration. In the end a really kind midwife came along and spent an hour getting the baby properly latched on so that she could feed. Only then did I feel some relief. And the soreness only lasted a couple more days.'

Marie, thirty-five, mother of Joanna, two

'The worst bit for me was walking around with leaking breasts for the next six weeks. Once I went into milk production the stuff just poured out of me. I could have fed the entire hospital ward and still had plenty left. It soaked through those pads you have to stuff into your bra and I'd look down to find two big round wet patches on my shirt. Parenthood comes with regular humiliation. Cue to grab the baby and pump it full of milk yet again in order to buy myself a wet-patch-free hour before the leaking began again. I ended up with the fattest baby you've ever seen; no problem, luckily, because breast-fed fat is different and does drop off, but the poor little thing looked like a miniature sumo wrestler for the first year.'

Sarah, thirty-three, mother of Molly, seven, and Josh, three

Of course there's always the option of cutting out the breast-feeding and heading straight for the safety of formula milk and bottles. We're all told 'breast is best', but life is sometimes just about finding out what works for us and breathing a sigh of relief.

I certainly found that after a few weeks giving my son a bottle was a welcome option, in fact the only option. For a start it was the quickest cure for an agonising bout of mastitis. But on top of that he looked into my eyes for the first time during his feed. I'd been told how wonderful this was and that it was one of the joys of breast-feeding. But since his nose was buried in my chest all he ever looked into was the weave of my jumper, while I waited hopefully for this glorious bonding moment which never arrived.

When he finally did look up, as I plugged the bottle in, I was never quite sure whether it was a glare of horror at finding himself on formula or not, but who was I to care? He'd looked at me and not just a glance either, he fixed his eyes on mine for what felt like ages, and it was the beginning of a bond that has gone from strength to strength.

And speaking of strength, while I didn't believe it for a long time, our bodies do recover – honest. Just don't expect it all to happen within hours or even days after the birth. It takes weeks before the physical effects of the birth wear off. So give yourself a break, plenty of warm baths, hot toddies and praise for getting this far and sit it out – just don't forget the rubber ring!

Baby bonding

The powerful mixture of our own expectations and society's pervasive influence results in the assumption that, following the birth, we will fall instantly and irrevocably in love with our children. But in reality this is by no means always a dead cert.

I know when presented with my son I was utterly amazed. I have never experienced anything like it, before or since. I couldn't believe that he had really arrived and that we were both okay. I'm not sure exactly what else I expected, but at that stage nothing else happened. I'd often heard parents describe how they would die for their children, but all I felt was tired and a failure for not feeling anything quite that powerful and all-consuming. I remember being awake all night after his birth and just staring at him in the cot next to me. My instinct was to pick him up in the hope that it would make me feel closer to him, but no one else seemed to be like-minded and I felt constricted by the apparent hospital attitudes.

Hours, or was it only minutes, later I had my first clarity of thought. I knew instinctively that if he never found out quite how scared I was and if I could stay just one step ahead of him that we'd be okay.

In reality, it wasn't until a few weeks in that we really began to bond deeply. But as time has gone on and each day, month and year have passed I'm constantly amazed by the depth of my love for him. Just when I think it would be impossible I become even more hooked, and today I would die for him without a moment's hesitation.

For the lucky ones the bonding happens straight away. But almost every new mum gets the baby blues, a bout of tears and confusion which usually sets in around the third day and lasts for a day or two at most.

> 'For the first three days after my baby was born I felt fantastic, on a high and very pleased with myself. I loved having people around, showing him off and telling the birth story. Then on the third evening I suddenly felt terribly low and couldn't stop crying. It was as though I went into shock and it hit me just how much my life was going to change. Everyone was kind, but I felt no one understood how awful I felt. Luckily it passed after about twenty-four hours and I felt okay again, but it was scary while it lasted and I wouldn't wish it on anyone. One of the midwives told me I had the baby blues and that it was very normal, especially on the third day after the birth. She told me to have a good cry and it would soon be over. I didn't believe her, but she was right.'
>
> *Sue, twenty-nine, mother of Ryan, one*

'I was so lucky, I bonded instantly with both my babies. There was an enormous feeling of both shock and love. The first time I came out from underneath the sheet, where I'd hidden throughout the birth, I was just flabbergasted. There he was and I fell instantly in love. The second birth I was terrified I'd have another boy and was so keen to have a girl that I was really quite scared of how I might react if it wasn't. Fortunately she was, and I never had to cross that bridge. Again it was instant love. Baby blues? I remember crying on the first night with my son, just feeling that I was a mum now and being staggered by how overwhelming that was. The second time around I wasn't upset or tearful at all. It was almost as though it was better the devil you know and I hadn't got to be scared about anything this time around. I just felt overwhelmingly tired, but didn't stop to cry as the hospital staff were telling me to go home after three hours and I just felt as though I wanted to sleep. I've paid my dues all my life and hadn't got my money's worth from the NHS, so rather than crying I argued them into letting me stay one night!'

Robina, thirty-three, mother of Christopher, five, and Jessica, two

'Bonding was thankfully immediate and I can only say it was akin to falling in love all over again, which can't be bad. I loved my son from the second I saw him and soon realised that the one thing they'd overlooked at ante-natal classes was to tell you how to get rid of the crick in your neck from constantly looking down and smiling at him! I did get the baby blues for a day or two and cried constantly, but when I got home I realised there was worse to come. I got the husband blues as well. He had failed to set the cot up properly and hadn't got the house exactly as I wanted it. Perhaps it was the baby blues still, after all. When I look back on that time and at all the treasured photos I can't help thinking that nature does take care of itself. Today I have a good-looking child. Then I had an ugly baby, the kind with a face a friend pointed out recently – and only a very close friend could say this – that only a mother could love!'

Sheila, forty, mother of Sean, three

'It was instant. A great feeling of being completely and utterly in love. Perhaps it was the relief that I had given birth to a baby and not a monster, that everything had gone okay and we were both safe, but all I felt from day one with each of my children was overwhelming love and a feeling of ecstatic happiness. I did get a bad attack of the baby blues a few days later though, I think when the exhaustion kicked in and I cried relentlessly for twenty-four hours or so. I was definitely unhinged around that time – it was a lot like having severe PMT.'

Laura, thirty-seven, mother of Joel, seven, Miles, five, and Nathan, one

Though my own experience was a bit more than just the baby blues I was fortunate in that it was nowhere near as extreme as postnatal depression. But for some women serious depression can set in after the birth.

If things get this bad then professional help is both needed and available. Just don't hesitate to ask for it, because there's lots available. There's no shame in asking for help, it's not a sign of failure, simply an act of courage and the only sensible thing to do. *WIPE!* may take a sideways glance at parenting, but antenatal and postnatal depression are very real and serious and are not a laughing matter. Thank goodness that they're resolvable and that help is available to disentangle the underlying physical, emotional or social causes. Life's too short and parenting potentially too fulfilling to miss one minute more than is absolutely necessary.

Parental panic

Strange how, regardless of the number of antenatal classes we have attended or the number of wise words we have digested pre-birth, before our offspring arrive there's no beginning to understand the degree of parental panic we are about to experience.

My personal panic, or perhaps paranoia, began before I even left the hospital. Having read about the meconium content to be expected in my son's first nappy, I was horrified by its appearance and firmly believed there was more to this than met the eye. No baby could possibly be healthy if this black goo had come from their system. It just couldn't be. Little did I know that this was perfectly normal and that before long I would become a world expert on every possible variation of nappy contents known to man. From yellowy orange while breast feeding, to a firmer pale brown when he took to the bottle – easier to negotiate but less pleasant on the nose – the whole business proved to be a science in itself. And the alarming regularity with which he appeared to be able to produce these substantial gifts was also a source of constant amazement. With every new tint and hue came a moment of panic that this time there really was something wrong.

> 'It was when my baby began to produce nappies full of something which looked like spinach soup that I began to worry. I'd kept cool through the black and yellow poo stages. But green! That was too much. Despite the fact that my child looked remarkably cheerful about it I became convinced she had some rare intestinal disorder and rang the health visitor, the breast-feeding counsellor, my mother and anyone else who would listen. They all patiently reassured me that it was perfectly normal and that I could probably expect her to produce several more variations on the colour theme over the next few weeks.'
>
> *Sally, twenty-seven, mother of Emma, four*

And as if producing all sorts of unknown matter from hell from one end wasn't enough, having a baby who could compete for awards from both did little to convince me all was well. The arrival of projectile vomiting can tax the nerves of even the most resilient of parents. The first time it happened was possibly one of the scariest parenting experiences to date. As my child's vomit impacted on a wall a few feet away, I expected his head to spin at any moment. This could not be physically possible. He could not be human. What had I bred? I became convinced that something must be seriously wrong. Surely no child, or adult for that matter, could possibly vomit in such a manner and survive. But apparently they can, and do, and often with alarming regularity. Positing small amounts of milk on my shoulder after a feed was horrible enough and did nothing for the state of my wardrobe, but vomiting on this scale was clearly going to require major redecoration.

> 'Projectile vomiting terrified me and I took a great deal of convincing, by both health visitor and GP, that my baby was really all right. The temptation at first was to call them each time he so much as hiccuped, and I was more than prepared to stay up all night downloading information from the Internet so I was armed with potentially useful facts for the medical profession should they need some assistance each time we called. But gradually I came to understand that this simply wasn't helpful! And, apparently, my baby was a little more resilient than I imagined. Over time I've learned to pause, take a deep breath, listen to and trust my instincts. Most of the time all is well and when he vomits I just keep up his fluid intake to avoid dehydration. But the bottom line will always remain: if in doubt call the doctor – it's better to be safe than sorry.'
>
> *Jane, thirty-six, mother of Tom, three*

Bathing my son, particularly after the high level of activity from both ends, was another terrifying task. I confess to 110 per cent terror of this particular parenting requirement. He was already as wriggly as a miniature eel; add soap and water and it would clearly become impossible not to drop him. I couldn't begin to imagine how we would ever manage. Getting all the necessary kit together – a breeze. Ensuring the bathroom and the water were all the correct temperature – a walk in the park. Take one squirming baby, add soap, shampoo and water – an impossible feat. In truth, it took a good couple of months before my fear levels began to subside and I became confident enough to attempt this manoeuvre alone. And, at the risk of comparing him to a runner bean, topping and tailing was often as good as it got when home alone. Bath time finally, and thankfully, became a pleasure once he was old enough to be contained in a securely attached and enclosed bath seat. For once, he was completely clean and we were both happy.

But once out of the bath we immediately entered the world of fashion hell. Pre-birth I naïvely assumed that dressing my son would be one of the fun parts of early parenting. How wrong could one insanely exhausted mother be? Would he be too cold? Would I accidentally overheat him? At every turn there appeared to be a staggering number of ways in which I could unintentionally harm my child.

'One layer of clothing more than you,' the health visitor helpfully advised. Considering I resemble some form of reptile and consequently permanently dress for Siberia this didn't bode well for judging appropriate levels of attire for my son.

And the problems didn't end there. Once I finally had the situation just about under control it'd be time to leave the house for yet another packet of nappies and I was apparently required either to develop all the meteorological skills of Michael Fish or resort to carrying an industrial case full of options for every possible weather eventuality from woolly hats to factor 20+.

'My first baby was born in December and I was so anxious about keeping this tiny creature warm that I overdid it by about six layers. He was so swaddled that it was hard to find the baby under all the jumpers and blankets. But when my sister called round and we dug him out from inside it all he was almost at boiling point and his face was scarlet. After a lecture from her about the dangers of overdoing it I eased off on the woolly blankets and eventually found the right level, so that he could breathe easily and so could I.'

Marion, thirty-nine, mother of Luke, seven, and Callum, five

At the end of a long day battling bizarre medical bombardments and freak weather conditions at least there would be sleep. Or rather there should be. In your dreams. What I simply hadn't bargained for was being so exhausted following the birth itself that I was a long way from catching up, much less living a life feeling somewhere close to well rested. At the end of a long day my sensible self told me my son should be placed lovingly but firmly in his cot to sleep and only be fed perhaps once or twice a night. It would only be a matter of weeks before we achieved a straight eight hours a night. The real me, however, was so exhausted that having my son in bed with me was the only practical option available. Besides, with a newborn came the additional parenting paranoia of having to check he was still breathing at least every two minutes and if that was going to become the absolute necessity it was proving to be, for my own peace of mind if nothing else, then surely it had to be easier when it didn't involve having to drag myself out of bed!

So why did I exhaust myself still further by wasting time struggling to work out how to become the perfect parent, and loading the guilt on to myself for the less-than-perfect decision I had already made? Admittedly, six years on he's still coming in and out of my bed but what the heck! The nappies didn't last for ever. The bottle feeds stopped when he was – eventually – ready. And I do believe, really I do, that he won't still be doing this at eighteen.

> 'We had our daughter in bed with us from the beginning. She was happy, I was happy and my husband was, if not exactly happy, at least tolerant. I could feed her without getting up, check on her when I needed to and feel her warm little body close to me. But my son was a different story. I brought him into our bed, but after a week we gave up and put him in his cot. He kicked and wriggled so much that none of us slept. After that we just kept the cot next to our bed and it seemed to work better.'
>
> *Jean, thirty-four, mother of Sorcha, five, and Sean, three*

So much for sleep. But what to do when your baby not only doesn't sleep, but cries relentlessly? The books touch on it, no doubt the antenatal classes I failed to attend did too, but I was supposed to have the perfect baby not a fractious little creature who, from time to time, showed no means of being placated. I have to say I was lucky. My son rarely went through these phases but when he did it was capable of driving me to new levels of distraction, dismay and dementia. When hunger, wind, comfort, nappy changes and checking for all obvious signs of illness had been covered, only two possibilities remained. Either something was seriously wrong or he was simply out to get me. Nature craftily designed a baby's cry to provoke a response from us. And design-wise it's spot on. Unfortunately, nature failed to design me with the ability to ascertain with any speed what my son might have needed when it didn't fall neatly into my automatic checklist. At such moments it was easiest to blame myself. I was clearly a bad, and somewhat inadequate, mother, the maternal monster of my darkest nightmares.

> 'Some days it got so bad that rather than damage myself or my daughter in any way I was forced to resort to putting her safely in her cot before closing the door, going into another room, howling and then calling a friend to ask for help and a much needed sanity break. I felt like the most hopeless mother in the world. Everywhere I went there were pictures, adverts, images of happy and smiling parents and babies and here I was with a child who, despite my best efforts, did nothing but cry for hours on end. But you know what, it happens to us all at some time or another, and despite what my head might lead me to believe from time to time I'm not special or different – just a parent experiencing real parenting.'
>
> *Anne, thirty-two, mother of Lucy, one*

The truth about those few weeks after the birth, as any mother will testify but few experts will admit, is that they're messy, confusing, anxiety-making and exhausting. And anyone who emerges from them without having become a neurotic deserves a medal.

Wipe wisdom

- Before the birth empty the freezer and stock up on frozen veg at all costs. Following an episiotomy sit on them (preferably wrapped in a cloth to avoid ice burns). It helps!

- Lift nothing except the baby for as long as you can get away with it.

- If at all possible marry a man with a fat bank account and a fully staffed household.

- Prepare yourself for the baby blues with a huge box of tissues, comfort foods and anyone who'll listen patiently to you sobbing about how overwhelming it all is.

3

Hitting the Big Time

Why your body may never be quite the same again

So you made it past those first few chaotic weeks, learned which end of the baby is which, expelled more bodily fluids than you thought possible and actually managed to sit in a chair again without the indignity of wobbling about on a child's buoyancy aid. Congratulate yourself for having got this far and then breathe deeply before you read on.

Thought that was it? That the next step was back to normal, back to the old, familiar you? Sadly it's time to let go of that particular little fantasy. Because you will never, ever be the same again. Not just because your ear will be so finely tuned to the slightest bump in the night that deep sleep becomes a rare luxury. Not just because getting out of your front door now takes approximately half a day, or even because every decision now involves an extra person. No, the changes I'm talking about here are the ones that mean the body you used to know so well is now transformed into a brand-new body which you'll have to get to know all over again, with different needs, different requirements and, in all likelihood, a very different shape.

Fat is the new thin

How is it that having lost the weight of the baby, amniotic fluid and the placenta, we still manage to look several months pregnant? There is no justice. Just like there is no return of the pre-pregnancy figure immediately after childbirth, or perhaps ever. Unless, possibly, you're a supermodel with vast levels of wealth and willpower. And even then there are no guarantees; supermodels have been known to turn up on beaches with dimpled thighs and less than flat stomachs, although not often, I admit.

But if you're heading into a blind panic don't lose heart. My figure did return. It just wasn't the one I recognised from pre-parenting days, but I've learned to live with it and even love it again – with time!

> 'My figure? I'm still fat as a house. The first pregnancy I got slimmer during the pregnancy itself and came home in my old clothes with a fabulous bust. This time, four months later and I'm still in maternity clothes. Now my fab bust feels like it's destined to be an old woman's bust – the kind you have to carry round with you. I'm just glad I'm married to a man who's been married before. If I was wife number one he might just think he could do better, but the husband on round two at least knows how expensive it would be to get rid of you.'
>
> *Jo, forty-six, mother of Sam, three, and William, four months*

> 'I was desperately skinny after the birth of my first child, which I hadn't expected at all, so that was a nice surprise.

The only disappointment was when I assumed it would be the same with my second. I put on weight and looked like an avocado pear for a long time afterwards. There's just no telling what it's going to do to you.'

Lucy, forty-one, mother of Maisie, four, and Daphne, two

'I lost weight when feeding my first but then put it on with my second which, although common, doesn't make me feel any better about it! Starving would be an option to get my figure back, but instead I just walk a lot, and pushing a double buggy with my third child attached on a skateboard has given me biceps if nothing else.'

Jeanne, thirty-five, mother of James, four, Lewis, two, and Daisy, six months

Childbirth takes its toll, and not just on our figures. Inexplicably the rush of hormones seems to carry with it a risk of our fashion sense leaving by the window too. Overnight, women who once wouldn't have been seen dead in a floral floaty number or a giant pair of dungarees become perfectly happy to walk, or waddle, around in public in clothes that could double as curtains in the local Women's Institute.

So how do we get our fashion sense back on track? I feel a campaign to ban leggings after the birth, or even during pregnancy, has to be a good place to start. There is little to be said in favour of stretching Lycra over an ever-expanding figure.

All floral or sailor numbers should also be actively discouraged. Where chain store fashion buyers get the idea that such outfits are a good idea, or remotely flattering, escapes me.

And finally, dungarees. Our children may develop a passion for Bob the Builder but it's important that, despite any hormonal changes, we retain a balanced perspective on life and remember that we are embarking on parenthood, not careers as CBBC characters.

While I recognise that it's not always possible or even affordable to look glamorous, elegant or sexy every moment of early motherhood, save your worst fashion moments for when you're very definitely alone and there's no danger of getting caught in the act. However much the father of your offspring may worship the ground you walk on there are limits beyond which it is unfair to push a man and this must be recognised as one of them.

> 'I stopped caring what I wore for the first few months after the birth. In fact I felt it was something of an achievement to get into any clothes at all. I spent half my days trotting round the house in my outsize pyjamas. When I did manage to dress myself, in one of the brief intervals when my baby stopped screaming, I was happy to drag on the nearest pair of jeans (stretch) and a T-shirt (baggy) and leave it at that. Then one day I caught sight of myself in a mirror and shuddered in horror. Who was this shapeless, balloon-like woman? That was it, time for a clear-out.'
>
> *Jane, thirty-six, mother of Tom, three*

> 'I cringe at the thought but have to confess to wearing a white T-shirt dress while I was pregnant, which stretched to the limit over my bump and finished off with two rara frills round the bottom. With great big yellow, red and

orange flowers all over it. I really don't know what I was thinking of! I didn't actually wear it again after the birth (it had stretched beyond hope), but I carried on wearing plenty of my other maternity clothes for months. Big mistake: not only did they look awful but they disguised how fat I still was and I got a horrible shock when I realised just how many rolls of blubber I still had to shift. My top tip would be a radical change of hairstyle to distract from everything else.'

Jenny, thirty-six, mother of Jasmine, seven

Which brings me to the next cardinal rule of post-birth dressing. Don't wear your maternity clothes. They do absolutely nothing for us during pregnancy and are definitely best given to charity or pregnant friends immediately after the birth. After which a couple of hours out from the endless round of feeds, changes and mopping, to buy ourselves a couple of outfits which remind us of the women we used to be is a definite must.

A quest for some breasts

You've either got it or you haven't. Cleavage, that is. God supplied me with one for most of my adult life and very nice it was too, but foolishly I took it for granted. Then I had a baby and it got even bigger before I waved it goodbye and we parted company for ever. I distinctly remember the shock of getting a figure back, post-childbirth, only to discover that it wasn't mine. From a 36B to a 36AA. Where did they go?

Bosoms, breasts, boobs, call them what you will, have

become a symbol of sexuality. Then all of a sudden, upon the arrival of children, they're put to their original, intended use and it's a whole new set of rules. From objects of desire they expand, without the help of technology, only to become objects not to be produced in public to feed your child, for fear of causing offence. A symbol of sexuality versus their original objective. The two clash. No wonder I'm confused. And then there's the size issue. Post-childbirth your size can change so many times that no sooner have you left the bra department than you're back again, begging for bigger, smaller, wider, narrower. Forget colour and style, you're just grateful to have anything that will fit.

After my son was born my breasts were so huge that whatever I wore I couldn't get away from looking every bit the dairymaid as I poured out of everything. Now I understand why huge, baggy sweatshirts are in alarming abundance in maternity fashion.

Then there was the time, a few weeks later, when I developed mastitis, preventing me from feeding him on one side. I will never forget, or indeed live down, my first night away from my newly acquired small attachment. I 'expressed' from the non-affected side before leaving the dairy and went out with a matching pair, only to watch my right side increase, continue to increase and increase still further over the course of the evening, until the company I was in could barely contain their shrieks of hysteria and eventually failed to resist at all, as my breast established its efficiency as a pint glass stand for the remainder of the evening. I arrived home that night a few minutes after my right boob had entered the house and shortly after decided to abandon all efforts to bond with my baby through breast-feeding.

Big mistake. End of breast-feeding, end of breasts as I knew them. I watched in horror as they shrank to nothing and then shrank still further. Immediate action was called for. My mission: a Wonderbra. However, things went from bad to worse during the fitting. I stood, mortified, as the sales assistant openly tittered when even the smallest cup size failed to come anywhere near my skin. After that it was either surgery or the children's department. Financial considerations won the day and I returned home the proud owner of a red tartan padded training bra.

Over the years I have regained confidence and returned to ransacking bra departments, but I still keep a sensible distance from fitters. Today, although I remain confused by the apparently contradictory 'push-up and plunge' bras and frankly just scared by those offering 'the biggest cleavage ever', I have finally found a padded, push-up number that actually fits. It's Rigby and Peller for me, the middle ground between surgery and cheap, department store degradation. Nobody laughs and it only requires a small second mortgage to be pushed up, pulled out, or plunged.

While I miss my cleavage, though these days I can fool people from a distance of no less than ten feet, I suspect it's even harder for the well-endowed. The only bra options available claim to offer 'the ultimate in comfort' while appearing to spread it all out and hide it under your armpits. Just how comfortable is that?

'I had quite a big bust before I had my children and I was rather proud of it. Sexy cleavage was one thing I wasn't short of, and I had plenty of low-cut little numbers to show it off. But after the kids? Oh my God. My bust looked like a sack of potatoes; no, make that two sacks of potatoes. And it weighed about the same as two sacks of potatoes. The only bras I could wear were so unflattering that I cried when I got them home. But at least they gave me a bit of support. I was seriously considering reduction surgery when, a few months after I stopped breast-feeding, my breasts finally started to shrink. Now I'm still big, but at least I can get into sexy bras and walk upright without back strain.'

Maggie, thirty-five, mother of Sarah, six, and Rory, three

What I did learn in my endless find-the-right-bra investigations is that it's important to find a bra that fits properly. Badly fitting bras can lead to pain in the neck (I can think of more obvious causes), back, shoulders and arms, compression of internal organs and strain left, right and centre from bra-strap syndrome.

So don't give up, the right bra's out there somewhere. And as for our new boobs, whatever size they happen to be right now, perhaps the best, and possibly only, option is to learn to love them, just as they are.

From top to bottom

As if the pain of childbirth wasn't enough, the knock-on effect appears to be that certain parts of my body, if not my life, have decided to head south. On the rare occasions I'm daft enough to look in the mirror, I'm left asking which is dropping faster, my self-esteem or my buttocks.

And not only is it shape, but texture too. I've got stunning dimples, they're just not where dimples ought to be. The only consolation lies in a wise decision not to tattoo my left cheek with a daisy chain, which would by now resemble a relief map of Africa. Even my five-year-old began asking what my 'extras' are for. I realised it was time to weigh up my options. Never undress again, or exercise. In a vain attempt to hold it all together, or rather to hoist it all back up, I enthusiastically opted for the latter. Then real life kicked in. I have little time and even less inclination to hurl myself around vigorously for long-term results; instant gratification's more my thing. Which is why I'm still sagging and I never did make it to the gym. Great. Another two reasons to feel bad about myself and ladle on the guilt.

Thankfully, however, on an amble around good old Marks and Sparks, the shape of things to come altered dramatically. Support knickers. No, they're not covered in affirmations designed to improve our self-image, but improve our self-confidence they do. A million questions flashed through my mind. Will there be bulges at the join between my Big Sensible Pants and real life? Where could the excess possibly go, and what about my circulation? But with new-found enthusiasm and hope for my plummeting posterior I set off in search of the best the world had to offer in BSPs.

What fun! I'd recommend it to all mothers with time on their hands. I struggled in and out of changing rooms, trying on one brand of ample bloomer after another. Up to my neck, down to my knees and everywhere in between. I'm ashamed to admit that all were an improvement on nature, but most were so deeply unattractive that they'd have to be stunningly effective to persuade me to risk passing out in them.

I finally found the pair for me, and these days I'm very attached to my BSPs. This may, of course, be to do with their vice-like grip, but they also conjure up memories of those compulsory, grey flannelette school knickers which we used to call Passion Killers. I appear to have come full circle. My grandmother would call these Harvest Festival Knickers and she'd be right. All is safely gathered in, thank God, and long may it stay that way.

'That layer (or six) of fat which everyone swore would drop off the minute I'd had my baby not only didn't but it multiplied into a few more layers in the months after the birth and, despite all my efforts, it had clearly decided to stay glued to my hips for life. I went swimming a lot, which at least firmed up my fat, but after that it was a question of learning to live with it. Comfy knickers and flattering skirts helped a lot. I even came to like the new, curvy me. It just wasn't how I'd imagined myself and it took a bit of getting used to.'

Liz, thirty-seven, mother of Jack, ten, Sam, seven, and Ben, four

'I've decided there are two types of women. The ones who get back their figure after a baby and the ones who don't. Along with about 90 per cent of the female population I come in the latter category. Generally how this works is that what you lose on your boobs miraculously reappears, trebled, on your bum. Isn't nature wonderful! So what do you do then? Begin a lifetime's struggle with diets which don't work, or give in, go up a couple of clothing sizes and get comfortable with the new, differently sexy, you. No choice really.'

Janet, forty-one, mother of Susie, twelve, and Molly, seven

So there you have it. A whole new, previously undiscovered, undergarment for the new you. Now wasn't that worth all the traumas of childbirth?

Sex after childbirth – just don't wake me

Sex? Gosh, yes please, particularly as I've just given birth. Sound familiar? I thought not. For once the textbooks proclaiming that sensual massage is enough may have a point. You can't wriggle out of the pain of childbirth, but when it comes to resuming your sex life you do have a choice and you can dictate the pace.

So, as primal instincts begin to resurface, just what can we expect? Cross your legs for a definitive guide to resuming your sex life after a baby.

Will it hurt?

Frankly, yes. Even without complications the perineal area can feel bruised and sensitive. Go carefully, gently and very, very slowly.

Just how long must 'sensual massage' be enough?

Just as long as it takes. Doctors say wait six weeks, but

some women aren't ready at six or even twelve weeks. Let all wounds heal and stitches dissolve before resuming intercourse.

What if he can't wait?

I'm sorry, but he'll have to. But do make sure you make time for each other between feeding, nappies and relentless screaming (the baby's, that is). Talk to each other – and listening's not a bad idea either. In time, after the ultimate in shared experiences, sexual utopia could be yours. Remember at this point that it's quality not quantity. Or so I'm reliably informed.

> 'I got things completely inside out and thought the doctor said we had to have sex before six weeks, not after. So I got really anxious and kept telling my husband we ought to do it, even though I didn't really feel like it at all! We did, just before the deadline, and thank goodness it was okay, though I have to admit not the most rapturous sex we've ever had. After that I relaxed and our sex life gradually got back to somewhere near normal by about three months after the birth.'
>
> *Bridget, forty-two, mother of John, eleven*

Eventually, of course, you will get your sex life back, but, like your body, it may not be in a form you recognise. A wild, exciting, spontaneous sex life and small children don't often go together, though there are notable exceptions so you can always live in hope. For most of us it's a question of temporarily suspending our sex life and then reinstating it, or rather slipping it back into our lives between bouts of exhaustion and endless nappy changes.

> 'Unlike most of the other things in my life I have always felt stunningly uncomplicated about sex. When I first met my husband life was pretty wild and carefree. Life was full of sensual pleasures, hedonistic delights, laughter and love. We got up at lunchtime and went back to bed in the afternoon for sex followed by dreamy, slothful sleep. Sex could be urgent, spontaneous and passionate or slow, sensual and indulgent. Then we had three children!
>
> 'A friend of ours, with four of her own, urged us to: "Go out as often as you can, enjoy each other fully, it'll be different when you have children." At the time I didn't really understand what she was trying to say. Of course we would still go out when we had children. Perhaps I would have understood more if she'd said: "Shag each other whenever you want to, wherever you want to, because you sure as heck won't be able to when small people arrive. They'll be with you from six in the morning until at least six at night and then at various times through the night as well."
>
> 'We had three children in four years. No more afternoon lovemaking, or certainly not without being interrupted by shrieks, exploding nappies and vomit. Our bed has become an instrument of torture rather than of sensual pleasure. We collapse into bed exhausted, desperate for sleep rather than sex and just as we begin to fall into a luscious, deep coma we're violently awoken by loud screams.

'Then the torture really begins. In this sleep-deprived state we're somehow expected to perform numerous, apparently necessary, tasks. Babies need feeding and winding before they're fully prepared to vomit all over you and your bed in appreciation. Then it's back to feeding again. Too tired to move ever again, the cot seems too far away and the baby falls asleep between us. Then child two develops a temperature and adds sticky Calpol to the bedtime equation. Inevitably we're then joined by child three who wouldn't want to miss out on the proceedings. But being kicked in the face and rolled on is a small sacrifice worth making for a well child, a happy one and a contented baby. Particularly if it means we might get some sleep. Finally. So sex, as you can see, is pretty much – temporarily, we hope – out of the equation. How different life is from those child-free days – it's not worse, just different.'

Georgina, thirty-seven, mother of Susie, five, Jenny, three, and Meg, one

'Sex after my first child can only be described as horrific. So bad was the damage to my body after the birth, in fact, that I had to be operated on six months later to be, effectively, rebuilt. It wasn't good and the knock-on effect on our sex life was a strain on us both. I think, having two children now, that it takes about two years for a woman's system to get back into gear. Quite apart from the damage, I was so tired for the first few months that I never wanted to see a willy again.'

Fiona, thirty-nine, mother of Jamie, seven, and Maddie, five

'It took six weeks before my husband got near me. That was what the hospital advised so I played on it, because sex was the last thing on my mind. This was my legitimate rest period and no one was going to persuade me otherwise! We did finally do it again and although it wasn't particularly painful it was like the first time all over again – probably because I was so obsessed with not being incontinent that I took pelvic floor exercises to a new level! Then we went back to once a week, once a fortnight if I could get away with it. Childbirth just put me right off it and now I'm just too tired.'

Clare, mother of Joshua, five, and Sam, two

So how are things from the men's perspective? After all, their sex lives have changed beyond all recognition too.

'Childbirth did put a damper on things for a while. My advice would be to get it while you can because afterwards – forget it. I had to understand that my physical needs just weren't my wife's priority at that time. She didn't know mentally, physically or emotionally if she was coming or going. When we did make love again I remember slightly resenting the fact that childbirth had changed her physically. It felt very different.

'Men are pretty simple creatures. When a woman becomes pregnant then effectively, in Darwinian terms, our role is over. It's not great feeling that way, if you stop to think about it and that's what made me behave like a child from time to time. Sex is the one thing we crave to make us feel part of and whole as a couple again and it's the one thing that's fundamentally affected. So the irony is that the very thing you need is the very thing that you can't get. But it does settle and all come around. I think it takes a woman years to readjust and acclimatise to her new role and as a man you just have to be patient. It took me years to readjust too, really. Eventually those close times do become available to you again in a very, very lovely way. It's just up to the man to put aside your greedy and needy head and remember that you get what you give. I get paid back a hundredfold for honesty and communication.'

Ben, thirty-seven, father of Tom, seven, Jake, four, and Tish, one

Normal sex life? What's that? The truth is it's whatever works for you and there's absolutely no need to feel guilty or worried. If you're swinging from the chandeliers again then great, although you might consider ringing the *Guinness Book of Records* as, believe me, you're pretty unique. But if you're so tired that all you can summon up when it comes to the subject of sex is a strangled laugh, then relax, you're not alone!

Wipe wisdom

- Top tip for looking good again: get your teeth bleached. The dazzling smile should detract attention from any parts of you you'd rather not display to the world. And if Joan Collins has made a career out of teeth and cleavage, why not the rest of us?

- Get off the guilt merry-go-round. Accept it's a myth

that you'll return to the gym on a regular basis and just concentrate on pelvic floor exercises. There's no excuse for being both saggy and incontinent.

- Don't dislike your body and try to hide it. Just accept that once you become a parent and get older and wiser you get sexier in a different way.

- Take a break from Lego and playdough and go and buy yourself something you feel gorgeous in; just make sure it's wipeable.

- Beat exhaustion by making time for each other while your baby naps.

- When you're finally ready to launch yourself from the chandeliers again, remember that Vaseline isn't just for the baby.

4

Leader of the Pack

How your relationships, with just about everyone, will change

Apparently it isn't just our bodies and sex lives which morph into something completely different following a new arrival. Having a baby makes a deep impact on almost all our relationships, blood or otherwise. So brace yourself for a whole heap of changes, negotiations and adjustments which will crop up between you and your partner, your parents, your in-laws and your friends. There probably isn't a single relationship that will remain exactly the same. But while some feel the strain and don't survive, others make it, and even flourish in the post-baby spotlight. Personally I lost a partner and a couple of godparents along the way but did manage to gain many, and varied, new friendships as time has gone on.

The long and winding road – back to romance

You both wanted this baby, you went through it all together and now you're both going to parent your treasured offspring together. Well, that's the ideal theory, anyway. But even in this, relatively rare, perfect scenario an awful lot of adjustment and change will be going on.

Who does what, how do you both feel about two becoming three – or four, or five? Is there ever time to talk, time for romance, time just to get away and be yourselves again? Dream on, I'm told by my married and cohabiting friends, is the appropriate response at this stage.

Certainly in my case we never reached the rosy, post-baby, deeper-bond stage which, for the lucky few, is supposedly possible. We made it, in an exhausted stupor which precluded all civilised conversation, through the first couple of years, before we had to admit that there wasn't much of 'us' left, certainly not enough to salvage.

> 'I thought we'd have this amazing shared experience and ultimately a deeper relationship because of it. But while we have, over time, got the latter, the shared experience was a different story. We both adjusted to the baby at such different paces and I think for a long time my husband felt jealous of our child and often ended up behaving like one himself as a result. On top of that, whilst I could see what was going on with him, I found it very hard to give him the time and attention he'd had before and still apparently needed. I was completely at the mercy of my new baby, hormonally challenged and learning how to deal with the tidal wave of feelings which had hit me. As the months wore on it got easier in many ways, but I still find it so hard to be financially dependent and my husband finds it hard to be under so much pressure to bring in all

the money. The change from two people, two incomes, to three people and one pay packet has been difficult. Looking back on it I think we've just slowly learned to cope and to say what we need from each other in order to do that. That's certainly helped to reduce the rising level of resentment that we sometimes feel. We're both completely knackered and pushed to the limit, but we're getting there and definitely stronger for it.'

Barbara, forty-two, mother of Venetia, four

'Not calling each other Mummy and Daddy, particularly when the children aren't around, was a good decision! But it's still hard to remember that we're the same people we were before the children arrived. For a long time I could only see my wife as a mother and had consciously to remember how it used to be and that she was still the same woman I fancied and fell for before. For so long she was buried under nappies, stains and other such unsavoury child accessories. I definitely felt quite trapped once I knew we were having a family, but I suspect that's just an instinctive male reaction and you need just to get on with things to get past it.

'In many ways I think my wife tried to protect me from the middle-of-the-night tears, the tantrums, and, I suspect, a lot of daytime flare-ups while I was at work were kept secret. We talked about it later and she agreed that she did try to keep some of the "bad stuff" from me. Initially it was from fear that I might not stick around, as she'd been the one who wanted a family, but later it was just because we'd both got stuck in our respective roles.

'Communication does seem to be the key. When I guess

what's going on with my wife I'm inevitably wrong! Now that we're talking more about these things we're beginning to make some positive changes and to tell each other about what we find tough, as well as great, about having kids.'

Sam, forty, father of Max, five, and Sophie, three

'Since I had my three children I've had to learn that it's not possible to get all your needs met by one person. As a result I've built up a whole network of friends for support, so that my husband feels less overwhelmed. I resented not having his full attention at first, after the children arrived. We were both so busy looking after them, and exhausted, that it was hard to find time to meet each other's needs. Now, a few years down the line, I can see that I have to be more realistic, if I want to stay married, that is! Men and women are so fundamentally different anyway; even without the pressures of parenthood men can't meet all our needs. Often they don't even begin to recognise them, much less understand them! And I'm prepared to concede that it works both ways!'

Marion, thirty-three, mother of Jess, nine, Megan, six, and Josh, three

'After the children arrived everything was exactly the same. I really thought he might change, but he still went to the pub with his friends just as often and would disappear with his mates at weekends. That's probably the main reason why we split up. He definitely sees more of the children now we're apart than when we were together because now when he's got them at weekends he's got to be with them. He never took them swimming before, but he does now.

'It made me realise that a couple have to change and adapt together once kids come along or you just won't last the course together. If a man expects to go on leading exactly the same life he had before then he's not being realistic. I resented the fact that I made all the changes and he wouldn't make any.'

Sally, thirty-nine, mother of Becky, ten, and Susie, seven

'The impact on our relationship and on me was huge – all the truisms are true. I've never been through such a gamut of emotions before or since the birth. During the first period there was really very little that was positive; in fact if I'm honest it was almost all negative. I put a brave face on it, but it wore me down physically, mentally, emotionally, spiritually. On the outside I had a beautiful wife, children, home etc. On the inside I felt increasingly isolated. I felt irritated and had a vague sense of loneliness which sometimes went so far as a feeling of desperation and inner death. I loathed myself for feeling this. I had a huge resentment towards my wife and felt as though there had been some kind of female conspiracy. I thought if it wasn't for parenthood I'd be doing what I wanted in life. I'd be writing films and in Hollywood collecting my Oscar, but instead I was consigned to a life of domesticity. I felt enormous pressure to make money for the family and didn't seem to succeed there either.

'All of this, thankfully, has resolved with time. I came to realise that as a man I didn't really know who I was or what I was meant to be. I'm intelligent, hold down a job, got a 2.1 at university, everyone else got married and had kids but I didn't know what to do. I still feel that to a degree some days, but having made that realisation I am beginning to change. I think about what I need to do now to be a father and husband. It may be difficult and tough sometimes, but I know that if I devote energy to the benefit of my family I feel better about myself and then that makes me better towards them again. It's a self-perpetuating circle.'

John, thirty-eight, father of Mickey, five, and Grace, two

Next in line . . .

Within families the mere act of moving up a generation can knock everything out of kilter for a while. Personally it's done wonders for our family, although I confess to teething problems along the way. Feeling that my parenting skills were under constant scrutiny sent me close to insane on occasions, but once I developed enough confidence in myself and my ability to be a 'good enough' mother I found the often incessant remarks less painful. On more stressful days they still have the ability to grate, but nothing that a two-minute private rant wont cure.

I always vowed, in a petulant teenage manner, that I would never be like my mother. I'll never say 'such and such', I'd tell myself. Today 'such and such' comes out of my mouth with alarming regularity. Conditioning, I think, is the technical term. But far more importantly than that, I've learned to recognise that my parents do actually have valuable wisdom and advice to impart in certain, if not all, areas. And every now and again I manage to swallow my proverbial pride and listen. I think the best advice I received from a friend was to listen to what your parents have to say because they deserve that respect, then consider their advice and adapt it, or discard it, depending on what suits you and your children. Take what is useful and leave the rest. It's possible to disagree without being disagreeable, it's just a skill that has taken me some time to master. And I'm certainly still learning.

With in-laws it's pretty much the same story. If you got on well with them before you had children you'll still get on with them afterwards, though probably with a few extra irritations thrown in. If you loathed each other before, then kids may provide the bonding glue you need, though frankly it's more than likely that you'll still just go on loathing each other. But as they're your partner's parents and your children's grandparents we've got to do our utmost to make a go of it, haven't we?

'I'm very proud of my children. I think they're a reflection of how we've brought them up and the amount of love they receive. I'm also immensely grateful to my parents and my in-laws for not interfering and for the love they bestow on their grandchildren. My children have two sets of grandparents who are both alive and still married, which is remarkable in this day and age. For all their foibles and defects they are good people and lovely grandparents. I forgive them when they occasionally do tell me how to raise my children, in return for their support and stability and all they represent.'

Ben, forty, father of Johnny, five, and Hugo, three

'My advice to anyone where their parents or in-laws are concerned would be to say "yes, very interesting" and then do what you want. Don't bother having an argument over any opinions they might want to shove headlong at you, it's just not worth it. Parenting is too exhausting, without adding to the stress. My in-laws have, at various times, interfered when it came to feeding, breast-feeding routines, food: the lot, really. I think what helped us was the decision to stick to our routine rather than trying suddenly to adapt it to one they'd approve of when they came to see us. I tried that a couple of times and it just didn't work, the kids played up and I felt resentful. Now I just try to stay confident and do what I know works.'

Carole, thirty-four, mother of Jodie, eight, and Jasmine, five

'My mum is just so supportive, I think I'm exceptionally lucky. We don't have a lot to do with the in-laws and we never have had; in fact they never even saw my daughter until she was five months old. Thankfully with eleven brothers and sisters on my husband's side his parents are just too busy to bother much with us and I've successfully achieved an in-law-grief-free life.'

Davina, twenty-nine, mother of Gracie, six

'My mum interfered non-stop at the beginning, and although it was all well meant, it had the effect of making me feel useless and confusing me at the same time. And everything was a warning or a disaster story! It was all "Don't do that, you'll make the baby sick," or "Feeding her that often will make her fat/spoiled/demanding." I was on my own, so there was no one around to fend Mum off or back me up. It put a real strain on our relationship and I was relieved when, after ten days, she went home and I only had to speak to her on the phone.

'After that I just set about finding my own way to do things, with a bit of help from a breast-feeding counsellor and a few close friends who'd done it before – but a little more recently than my mum.

'In the end the whole experience was good for me because I became a lot more assertive with my mother and she learned to back off and let me do it my way. Today we have a much better relationship than we did before I had my daughter. I understand more about what she went through as a parent and she can see that actually I'm managing fine.'

Caroline, twenty-nine, mother of Suki, two

Friend or foe

I'd be willing to place money on the fact that we've all lost at least one friend to parenthood. And if you haven't so far it's almost bound to happen.

What I've found difficult at times is the impact becoming a mother has had on my relationships with childless friends. It's not something I ever considered or anticipated before my son was born. I just imagined that my friendships would roll on, the same as before. When I was pregnant I vowed not to become a baby bore and while there are times when I'd love to regale anyone who'll listen with endless stories about my son's incredible talents and exceptional abilities I know full well that I'd want to kill anyone who subjected me to similar torture. As a result I've made a conscious effort to keep my mouth firmly shut. But despite this my relationships with childless friends have suffered. Those who haven't had children have little understanding of the exhaustion, the new restrictions on time and freedom, the need for forward planning and my 110 per cent responsibility for someone else. And why should they? Except, of course, to accommodate me!

For me it's been hard to feel so much more cut off from my child-free friends. Take one of my closest girlfriends, Pam. Before my son's birth we had total empathy on both sides. Now there are huge gaps in understanding and lifestyle. She has no concept of my motherly ability to multitask while listening to her, or of the necessity, when we're talking, to stop mid-sentence while I prevent my child from destroying himself, or the nearest piece of furniture.

All this means that we now meet for cups of tea at ten at night, the only time my sitting room is almost guaranteed to be a child-free zone. And, though we've compromised, I think we both miss the closeness we used to have.

> 'I'm the child-free zone in this particular friendship and, if I'm honest, there are some things I really miss. Like our Wednesday night pizzas out. I'm none too keen on the idea that there isn't really a life for us now, apart from a once a week late-night cup of tea. I like Penny's son. But I do find it hard when she stops talking mid-sentence. That's dementing. It's just hard having a third person in the relationship, especially one who needs so much attention. I could cope better if she were nursing a comatose geriatric!'
>
> *Pam, thirty-seven, child-free zone*

'Single people find it really hard to understand parenting. They think they get it, but they just don't. Whatever you say, you can't really understand it until you have children. Lots of friends felt they'd lost us when we had three children in quick succession. We went from being extremely sociable to being up to our eyes in nappies. When we were still unmarried I remember my future brother-in-law and his wife having kids and thinking they were so dull because they were unconscious by ten thirty every night. But I hadn't a clue how hard it is!'

Sarah, thirty-three, mother of Jamie, five, Ben, three, and Ciara, six months

'After the children came along I became closer to my male friends who had children and drifted away from those who remained child-free. Some of them were very resentful. It was as though they felt I had somehow betrayed the male bond, the tacit understanding we should have between us, and I'd crossed to the other side.'

Keith, thirty-five, father of Molly, six, and Nat, two

'My closest girlfriend was fantastic when my first baby was born, even though she didn't have kids herself. She looked after me, arrived regularly with flowers and flannels and listened to me weeping about how hard it all was. I felt really lucky to have her around. There was never a problem about our relationship changing. It did, of course, but it adapted and we carried on together, just as close as we were before. And four years later, when she had her first baby, I couldn't have been more happy. It was my more casual friends who drifted away post-childbirth, the ones

I'd go to the pub with after work. I didn't mind that, they weren't deep relationships and probably wouldn't have lasted anyway.'

Beth, thirty-four, mother of Jo, seven

A gift from god?

Who do you ask? Why do you ask them? And where exactly is it that they disappear to? I can only assume there is a godparents' graveyard somewhere deep in suburbia that I wasn't privy to when making choices for my son.

My own three godparents soon whittled down to only one effective one, and even she only lasted until I was ten. So to be on the safe side, based on the percentage theory of loss, my child got five. Were they chosen for spiritual guidance or for the ability to care for him, should something happen to me? A bit of both, is probably the answer.

I chose from all walks of life, from liberal hippies to ardent football fans, in the hope that there'd be at least one he could turn to for advice. At the very least, with an expected drop-off rate of 60 per cent, he stands a better chance than I did of getting the odd card or birthday gift.

'We had godparents for both our first two sons. They were chosen specifically because they were old friends and therefore less likely to bugger off into the sunset. The difficulty was having an awful lot of old friends we didn't want to offend, so the boys ended up with five godparents each. Now we have a third son and we're so laid back about the whole thing that we haven't got around to choosing his yet, and he's two!'

Susie, thirty-five, mother of Daniel, eight, Alex, six, and Matthew, two

'I can barely remember who they are or which ones belong to which child! They were chosen because they were our best mates at the time, but we all drifted apart. I don't think I ever really expected anything of them, though, it was just a formality. Thinking about it, one godparent for each child has stayed. Perhaps a 33 per cent success rate isn't too bad these days. And top of the list is my sister, who'd have the kids at the drop of a hat if anything happened to me.'

Jennie, forty-two, mother of Claire, twelve, Hayley, ten, and Marcus, four

'I had problems with the concept of a church wedding and I struggled with the idea of godparents too. In the end I rationalised both issues on a lay basis, i.e. that they represented part of the fabric of this country, of which I was a part, so it was okay to do them.

'Having made the decision to have godparents it seemed important to have people we were both close to. I felt worried about asking someone to make a lifelong commitment to my children as this stated a lifelong intention on my part to stay friends with them and I'm a typical man who's scared of commitment. In the end all three children got three each, all very different and picked to complement each other. Spiritual versus pragmatic. Business versus the arts. In truth some have drifted a little, but my view is that they are for life and hopefully would be there if they were needed. If not I'd want to know why!'

David, forty-four, father of Fiona, seven, Josie, four, and Sam, one

Wipe wisdom

- If in doubt about godparents always opt for young and rich. That way they should live long enough, and be sufficiently well-off, to look after your kids in the style to which you would like them to become accustomed, should you somewhat carelessly fall under a bus.

- Don't expect child-free friends to fall in love with your baby – and don't bore them rigid with tales of your child's adorable antics, however strong the urge. Unless, of course, you want to lose them along the way.

- In laws: can make single parenthood seem strangely appealing, but try to avoid impulsive action you may live to regret.

- Partners: not dissimilar to the in-laws, but try to hold on to what you've got. Things do get better, or perhaps just different, or so I'm reliably informed.

- Childcare: think of it as a necessary hazard. To be approached with caution.

5

The Childcare Nightmare

Who do you trust?

Childcare. The word alone is enough to send shudders of horror through even the most seasoned of parents. Childcare: an unavoidable yet painful truth of parenting. And one we are often introduced to at a desperate and emotionally charged point in our lives, not least when we first have to return to work and leave junior in someone else's charge.

I've yet to meet a parent who can manage without childcare of some kind at some point. And most of us need it regularly right the way through our offspring's formative years. What we don't need, though, is the hassle, emotional turmoil, hideous choice-making (or in some cases lack of choice) and near-bankruptcy that childcare brings with it.

Nannies, au pairs, mother's helps, childminders, babysitters – which will it be? An assortment of several, perhaps, for different occasions? Especially as each one tends to stick to a very specific job description and they're loath to stray into each other's work territory. Or, in the case of most au pairs, any work territory at all.

Of all the changing relationships there are to deal with, post-childbirth, the ones with our childcarers, vital in order to maintain working life (and therefore pay said childcarers) will almost certainly be some of the trickiest to navigate. But navigate them we must, if only for our children's sake.

My own forays into the world of childcare first began when I decided it was time to find a regular babysitter who would provide me with the occasional worry-free evening out.

The problem, however, appears to be the guilt that came gift-wrapped upon my son's arrival, and which makes it extraordinarily hard to put my own needs first. Ever. Apparently a small but highly vocal committee lives in my head, arguing the effect on my son of every decision or move I might make, no matter how small. The committee members appear to have no time off, and when they do go quiet, lulling me into a false sense of security, I know it's only a matter of time before they're off again, niggling my conscience.

Bowlby's attachment theory – that children under three should be constantly with their mothers – has simply not been helpful to me or my peace of mind. I was somewhat comforted to learn that John Bowlby himself had a very pleasant childhood in which he was brought up by a nanny. And even more comforted to learn that his theory has now been discredited. But there remains for me the thorny problem of how to take a little time off for myself, without fearing that I'm psychologically damaging my child for ever.

When I was pregnant I conjured up the image of a

local granny figure who would adore my children and be adored by them. They'd then stay happily with her whenever Mummy needed a little break or had something pressing to do. But sadly no such granny figure emerged, scour the neighbourhood though I might.

My fears around unknown childcare were realised when, at around six months, I left my son for a much-needed evening out. The babysitter was a retired, well-spoken woman who'd been a paediatric nurse. Not too far off my granny image, in fact. I left a list of 3,000 instructions and then proceeded to spend the evening worrying and wondering whether she'd bothered to read my list.

When I got home I found my son wearing his nappy inside out and back to front. All very well if you're appearing on a bizarre game show. But this was my son she was experimenting on! The final nail was then firmly hammered into the coffin when she announced that he was lovely and next time she came she'd be tempted to take him out and keep him. I could have forgiven the nappy – they clearly didn't have disposable ones in her day – but child theft was going too far.

After a year or two of full-time motherhood I was given the opportunity of state-funded childcare, albeit for a very limited number of hours each week. Not enough to enable me to return to work, but enough to give me much-needed breaks. Even then I agonised about leaving him. How good, competent, caring, capable was this council-registered childminder? Frankly, anyone less than Mary Poppins was going to prove problematic.

But I took the chance, not least because I was struggling

for sanity throughout my son's illness and the breaks were quite simply a lifesaver. I remain staggered, however, at just how manipulative my son had become by that age. He knew just how to hit the guilt switch in me, and hit it hard. We would arrive, he would scream and cry, I would ensure he was safe, wish him a swift, confident goodbye and a cheerful 'See you later' and then listen outside the front door. Strange how the tears stopped and turned immediately to laughter the minute he heard the door close.

The live-in option

If your home is big enough and you can handle an extra person around the house all the time and you harbour a desire for substantially increased phone and shopping bills, then the live-in option may be a good one for you. Which basically means nannies or au pairs. Nannies tend to be qualified (though not always) and to do longer hours for more money. And they may or may not stay more than a week, dependent upon whether you have all the mod cons and holiday options they require. Au pairs, on the other hand, are relatively cheap and work reasonable hours, although they may well not have had any previous contact with children and may go into shock once this contact takes place. Added to which they may or may not speak English and may or may not do a bit of housework, as the mood suits them.

'If I'd wanted to have breakfast every morning with a nubile, bright-eyed but utterly thick Swiss nineteen-year-old I would have gone to finishing school. As it is I managed to avoid that particular pitfall, but it caught up with me when we employed an au pair to look after our two-year-old so that I could go back to work. Gretta was charming enough, and reasonably willing. She just couldn't get the hang of anything, not the iron, not the dishwasher, not the washing machine . . . So of course she couldn't do any work around the house. Well, we could live with that if she kept our toddler happy. And we thought she was doing just that, until the day I came home early to find Gretta in bed with her boyfriend (she seemed to have got the hang of how to do that okay) while our daughter was parked in front of a video. End of Gretta. End of au pairs. End of plans to go back to work until we managed to come up with plan B.'

Carole, thirty-three, mother of Jenna, two

'We always relied on au pairs to provide our childcare and on the whole it worked okay. We had a new one every six months, though occasionally one of the girls stayed on for a year. It always took a while to settle them in, and even then we had to act as surrogate parents, which meant keeping a close eye on their social lives and listening to their problems day in day out. But most of them did the job, got on okay with the children and stuck, roughly, to the rules we laid down. The worst time was when we discovered that the current au pair was HIV positive. With two small children in her care I felt scared. But would it be cruel or politically incorrect to get rid of her? Thank God the problem resolved itself. We were still agonising when she disappeared, leaving a note to say she wasn't happy and had gone home.

'Which nationality is best? Probably the Germans, though the French came a close second.'

Samantha, forty-two, mother of Daniel, fifteen, and Sarah, twelve

'Rosie was a really fantastic nanny – they do exist! We'd heard all kinds of horror stories from friends, so we were ultra-cautious when it came to finding someone to look after our own children. We wanted qualifications, references, trial periods and contracts! But Rosie proved to be everything we'd hoped for. The kids adored her, she worked long hours and was easy to have in the house. When the children started school and she had to leave we all missed her like mad.'

Kit, thirty-eight, mother of Gemma, eight, and Christy, six

'We decided to do up the spare room and have a live-in nanny, because we were both working unpredictable and sometimes long hours. We made the room lovely and offered what we thought was a reasonable and fair working package, with holidays thrown in. Three nannies later we realised that our nice but ordinary home and reasonable working conditions just didn't begin to compete with what was available out there. One nanny left to work for a mega-rich Saudi family, another was offered her own car and trips on the family yacht by some Americans, and the third went to work in a Scottish castle. Humbled, but not bowed, we kept on trying and finally hit lucky fourth time round, with a nice girl who was happy to stay, at least for a couple of years, despite the obvious lack of luxuries.

'The worst part was for the children, who seemed to lose a nanny just as soon as they'd got used to her. After a while we all became accustomed to seeing a different face at breakfast every few weeks.'

Sandra, thirty-six, mother of Lucy, six, and Kirsty, four

Or live-out . . .

Not so different from live-in childcare, except that at the end of the day the nanny, mother's help or childminder you employ goes back to their own home and you breathe a big fat sigh of relief and bolt the front door until the next morning when, bright-eyed, they're back on your doorstep. Or at least that's the theory. And of course there are obvious advantages. Your children are cared for in your own home, where they feel familiar and comfortable, and you know exactly where they are. You hope. And you don't have to deal with your childcarer's boyfriend/extra-marital/girlfriend problems in the evening when you're shattered after a hard day's work. Unfortunately, the disadvantages can also be abundant. When your childcare has to come to you, the situation is fraught with potential problems. They get sick, miss the bus, the trains were cancelled, they have to leave early . . . you get the idea. So whether they turn up or not is not dissimilar to your chances of winning the lottery. Only this time it's of the 'will I get to work today?' variety.

'Sharon was a really nice nanny who got on fantastically well with the children – when she was around. The trouble was that she wasn't around all that often. She was always asking for a day off for her sister's wedding or her boyfriend's job interview or her mother's illness. And then there was her own illness; she seemed to catch flu about every three weeks and disappear for a week. We were for ever taking days off work ourselves, or, in emergency situations, calling agencies to find stand-ins. Which wasn't what we wanted for the children at all. We wanted someone who'd be around for them most of the time. In the end we had to give up on her and find someone else. But that didn't work out either; none of us ever really gelled with nanny number two. Number three was fine, though. So I suppose I'd tell anyone starting out on this route that it's trial and error, but you'll probably get there and find someone you like in the end.'

Maeve, forty-three, mother of Laura, ten, and Sophie, seven

'I've had just about every nanny from hell that there is. First there was one who turned out to have a drug habit she'd forgotten to mention. I found her one evening looking glassy-eyed and out of it and when I realised what was going on I was horrified.

'Then there was the nanny who robbed me of almost £1,000 which I'd had in the house for some building work which had to be paid for in cash. I don't know how she knew it was there or how she found it. But the next day it was gone and so was she. I called the police but they never found her. She was Australian and I guess she'd headed home with her booty. I was left feeling shocked and betrayed and so was my son, who'd liked her. When the police investigated they found out that she had been living with a boyfriend, not far from us, and she'd robbed a couple of other households before me. I felt a complete fool, but her references had seemed genuine and she was charming. Now I'd say to anyone else, get verbal references as written ones may be faked. Make every check you can and even then be as careful as you can.'

Cara, forty, mother of Luke, twelve

'Lauren came to work for us as a mother's help and she was fantastic. We found her by putting an ad in the local paper. It's a bit of an old-fashioned title, but it suited what we needed, which was someone to help me out with three small children. I was around most of the time, which obviously made a difference, because I could show her what I wanted and keep an eye on her. But she was very willing and loved children and I felt very happy leaving any of them with her while I went shopping or got my hair done or had a cup of tea with a friend. She was only seventeen but she seemed to have a natural way with little children, perhaps because she had younger brothers. She stayed with us for a couple of years, until the oldest two had started school.'

Meg, thirty-nine, mother of Tania, seven, Beth, five, and Oliver, two

Childcare by numbers

Then there are childminders and nurseries, the choice for many of today's parents, not least, I suspect, because they fall into the vaguely financially feasible category. There are plenty of them around, but it can take months of mental torment to debate and decide on the one that is right for your child. Believe me, I've been there. And how on earth you can determine whether your child will get on with the two or three other children at the minder's, or twenty-five or so at the nursery is simply another stage of the torture.

Like everything else in the childcare world, it's a bit of a chancer. And after thoroughly checking out the premises, asking all the questions I could think of, both relevant and obscure, I then had simply to trust my instincts, before watching my son like a possessed hawk for any possible sign that he was less than 110 per cent happy and that all was not well.

> 'We chose the nicest nursery we could find. It was pretty, clean, well-organised and had friendly staff. But it was still very hard leaving our two-year-old there for the whole day. We needn't have worried, though.
>
> 'He loved it from the start. There have been a few dodgy moments, mind you. My husband got a bit worried when he turned up to see our macho little boy parading around in a purple dress one afternoon. Dressing up, it seems, is a favourite. Then there was the phase when he started to nick all the miniature dinosaurs from the nursery, stuffing them into his pockets and producing them when he got home. It got to the point where we had to frisk him when we picked him up each day.
>
> 'He's been at the nursery for two years. In fact they're like his second family now. I think he'll really miss them when he goes to school.'
>
> *Ailsa, twenty-nine, mother of Kieran, four*

'It took us about two months to settle our daughter at nursery. She was only going three mornings a week, but each time I had to stay with her for almost the whole time. She wouldn't move from my lap. If I tried to leave she'd start sobbing and clinging on to me and I couldn't do it. What persuaded her in the end was the water play. They had a huge sink they'd fill with water full of red dye, don't ask me why. It looked like blood, but Georgina loved it and would shriek with pleasure at the thought of rolling up her sleeves and getting stuck in. After a few days of this she was fine and she's never looked back.'

Sue, forty-four, mother of Georgina, three

'We trawled through the list of local childminders and just didn't know where to start. In the end we went round every one with a vacancy. Some of them were awful, really sterile and bleak and the women weren't especially sympathetic or child-friendly. After the first few I felt quite depressed and was sure we wouldn't be able to find anyone decent. But the sixth one turned out to be quite different. She was very warm and her home was bright, clean and full of toys and activities. We felt she was right for our daughter and settled for her straight away. And we weren't disappointed. Our daughter always went off happily and came home cheerful. It wasn't easy leaving her; it never got easy for me, even after a couple of years. But the childminder was brilliant.'

Jo, thirty-three, mother of Susie, five

The babysitter blues

Even when I was lucky enough not to be working and therefore had no need for daytime childcare, it wasn't long before I needed the occasional night out. And, unless among the lucky few who have willing grandparents on tap, welcome to the world of searching out a rare and precious breed, the reliable and trustworthy babysitter.

Unfortunately, there are absolutely no babysitting qualifications, no schools for babysitters or indeed babysitting academies. So once again it's back to trusting our parental instincts on this one. References help, but how many sixteen-year-olds come complete with those? And having tried many alternatives, word of mouth from somewhere along the local grapevine seems to be the best way to find a reliable babysitter. Preferably one who lives close by, so that remaining sober enough to drive them home at the end of the evening does not become a requisite, alongside the hard cash you will be required to hand over at the end of the night.

> 'We had the babysitter from hell. What was odd was that she looked like an angel, blonde, smiling and super-keen. But the minute we'd left she let her boyfriend and half her friends in and partied for the rest of the evening. We were horrified when we got home, particularly as we'd told her not to let anyone in. She was just too immature at sixteen to behave responsibly and we felt it was our mistake going for someone so young. After that we went through an agency and stuck to mature

women with children of their own. That got too expensive in the end, so we joined a local babysitting circle, which worked out fine. It meant that one of us had to babysit for another family from time to time, but in return we got free, trustworthy babysitters.

Vanda, forty-one, mother of Hannah, eight, and Rebecca, four

'We decided to get our kids used to babysitters early on and it really paid off. By the time he was three our son loved his babysitters – we had about three regular ones – and he thought it was a treat when one of them came over. We'd leave them to bath him and put him to bed while we escaped for an evening off-duty. They were all teenagers, but we didn't have any trouble at all. We always laid down the rules and made sure they could get in touch with us. We've got really nice neighbours who can be contacted in a crisis, so that reassured us too.'

Debbie, thirty-seven, mother of Julie, ten, and Robin, six

Anyone for a holiday?

The idea of taking a holiday is, I confess, one of my wildest fantasies. The idea of taking childcare with us, and being able to afford to do so, is when I know those fantasies are quite simply out of control. But if money's no object, or you throw caution to the wind, how do parents find the right person to frolic with their children in the waves while they relax on the beach? It's bad enough being stuck for two solid weeks with your own family. But with a virtual stranger . . .

'We took Katie, a seventeen-year-old daughter of friends of ours on holiday to look after our three-year-old. In the previous couple of years we hadn't had a minute off during the whole fortnight and it had felt more like a labour camp than a holiday. So we decided to try taking our own babysitter along. And Katie was brilliant. She shared a room with him, so that we could lie in some mornings. And she took him off to play on the beach for a few hours each day, so that we could lie around the pool reading and sunbathing. It worked for all of us. Our son loved Katie, she managed a holiday romance despite her childcare commitments, and we actually got a break and came home relaxed. Well worth the extra cost.'

Alison, thirty-eight, mother of Matthew, four

'Having been denied anything resembling a holiday for the years following childbirth and its subsequent loss of income, two balmy weeks in the south of France, indulging in all the pleasures of the flesh without having to expose too much of it, was tempting. Having then discovered that our all-singing, all-dancing tent had four separate zip-up compartments and could therefore, at a tight squeeze, accommodate ourselves, the two children and one other, we set about trying to find a way in which we might cajole someone to come on holiday with us and help out with childcare. With great mutual delight and anticipation, Kelly agreed to help us out in return for passage, bed and board.

'Alarm bells should have rung with the acquisition of fifteen cans of spaghetti. However, having never left the country before, Kelly's reluctance to eat anything at all bought in France was to some extent understandable. A cheap multipurchase you might think but there was an unseen price to pay.

'It was Kelly's first experience of seafaring. Too queasy to contemplate anything infant-related, despite a calm sea, Kelly was left to herself while, undaunted, we faced the fart-filled balloon pool in shifts and watched the repetitive magic show every hour on the hour. The rest of the journey to our first night's stop was uneventful, save for my son's trick of dropping off with one eyelid closed, the other open. This mildly freakish pose produced screams of horror every five minutes from Kelly, yelling, "That's disgusting, that is" – a phrase which became increasingly familiar.

'It was with some sympathy that we had endured Kelly's drawn-out version of unrequited love, so agreed to her phoning her beloved Matthew, albeit for a long-distance cold shoulder. We had obviously missed some vital link in Kelly's story as we learned to our surprise that Matthew was in fact a rabbit, Kelly's pet rabbit, with whom she had managed to hold a long and expensive telephone conversation.

'The starter of local rabbit pâté served up in a restaurant a few days later finally put paid to any preconceptions that Kelly might have had about us being caring, sharing individuals despite our desperate attempts to disguise it and prevent the children from learning the word for rabbit in French.

'Any notion of eking out a precious evening together was abandoned as Kelly, despite considerable encouragement to the contrary, had no desire whatsoever to leave us alone for a second. Night after night we sat wedged between canvas and our car at the plastic table with Kelly tucking into her tinned spaghetti and chips, while we guiltily consumed camembert which made her feel sick because "it stank", salami, which made her feel sick because it "stank", pâté . . . need I go on?

'I can honestly say that the climax (ho-ho) of our holiday came in the form of a reinvented sex life which took place entirely in the dark and without a sound so as to avoid waking up the snoring Kelly whose land of nod existed just millimetres away behind a polyester zip-up wall.

'The last day of our holiday was spent on our favourite beach, crunching sand-filled baguettes in a force nine gale. With a crazed determination to enjoy ourselves and sporting the latest trend in food-encrusted beach mats for warmth, the children assisted with their dad's rusty boy scout – or was it girl guide – attempts at storm shelters, announcing that there was no way that Kelly would fit in as she was too fat. Desperately hoping that her ears were, like mine, filled with sand and therefore deaf to the observant, if unkind prejudices of the children, I realised that her decidedly un-stiff upper lip suggested otherwise.

'On our arrival back home at three in the morning, Kelly's long-suffering parents arrived to taxi her home to find us unpacking outside in the rain in search of the elusive front door key, carefully tucked away so as not to be lost . . . or found. Finally inside, the children asleep, with a glass of Muscat in my hand, a holiday seemed like a really good idea.'

With grateful thanks to Victoria Page. Reproduced from WIPE *magazine*

So there you have it. When it comes to childcare there are absolutely no perfect answers. Just a stout heart, a strong instinct, a full purse and the ability to hang on in there until you find the right solution. Because, believe it or not, there always is a right solution. It just might take slightly longer to find than you hoped.

Wipe wisdom

- Never ask your nanny to do anything you wouldn't do yourself. On second thoughts, never ask her to do anything at all.
- Rest assured, four nannies by the time your child is out of nappies is not unusual. And at least two extra paid pairs of hands is not unheard of if you insist on having numerous children in dramatically quick succession.
- If your child hates the nanny, au pair, childminder . . . trust their judgement. Kids know.
- If your child loves the nanny, au pair, childminder . . . get out the champagne.

6

Sex and the Single Parent

The ups and downs of doing it on your own

Around one in five of us is doing it alone – bringing up our children, that is. And it can be a tough old road to travel. Rewarding? Of course. Worth doing? Naturally. Fun? Occasionally. But tough none the less.

We single parents – I joined the ranks when my son was two – do all the same things that dual parents do, the only difference being that we do them alone. But it's a big difference. We cope with illness, agonise about discipline, overdo and underdo things, see our young through nappies, teething and starting school. But doing it on your own can sometimes feel like double the responsibility and double the exhaustion factor. Never mind feel like, it IS double. Yes, we know that not all partners are shouldering their 50 per cent of the responsibility, or in some cases, any of it, but for single parents the total absence of another person who is even remotely likely to share in the parenting job can feel very lonely.

On the other hand there are things to be said for single parenthood. For a start I'm not trying to run an intimate adult relationship alongside parenting, a challenge which many parents in relationships have told me is occasionally akin to trying to run a marathon at the same time as climbing a mountain. But despite these off-putting sentiments, most of us single parents would like to be doing both, and from time to time we put what little extra energy we have after our kids' needs are met into looking for the partner of our dreams, though these days the criteria have shifted somewhat and he needs to be someone who loves kids, chores and domestic bliss, is never happier than when scraping tomato sauce off the walls and wants nothing more than to share in the upbringing of our little darlings, while playing romantic lead to us.

The dating nightmare

Two nights off each week: 104 opportunities a year. Give or take possible menstrual cycle interference and you're down to approximately eighty nights of passion per annum. Doesn't seem like much to me, but I'm assured by married friends that a figure like that is sheer indulgence.

So the problem merely remains finding an obliging partner whom I could perhaps even respect in the morning. Or, if I strike it really lucky, one with the unusual and rarely seen skill of mutating into a cooked breakfast overnight, thereby satisfactorily removing the need for either respect, conversation or cookery before negotiating the rest of my parenting day.

Dating is frankly a nightmare activity fraught with the

pressures of toenail painting, eyebrow plucking and, not least, the man himself – and is without doubt an occupation I had hoped to be finished with about fifteen years ago. But date I must, unless I resign myself to a lifetime of 'home alone' nights. But, let's face it, having a date these days is a miracle in itself. Where are all the eligible but not certifiable or seriously disordered men? I'm not sure I'm at liberty to divulge how many dates I have endured in these last four years of unparalleled freedom. Suffice it to say there have been some interesting times. Leaving me to conclude that most men are either emotionally unavailable, in need of more attention than my child, or simply dancing to the beat of a very different drum.

Last time I checked I wasn't in possession of a moustache or a small hump, so I can only assume that the problem is a locational one. Where to meet your perfect partner? The school gates? Not a huge dating opportunity. Supermarkets? Modern myth. Somehow my small child lying in the aisles in the throes of a tantrum doesn't enhance my sex appeal. Work? Personally I'm too knackered to get much work done, let alone pull on the job.

What's a girl to do? Perhaps simply grit her teeth, cross her legs, sprinkle bromide in her tea and resort to a hobby, at least until the offspring leave home. Only another decade or two to go. And if I'm past it by then, consolation lies in what a dab hand I'll be at flower-arranging. I'll be so busy at the WI that I may not even notice I'm single.

But the truth remains that while today I can spot a fairytale at a hundred yards, I'd be lying if I said I wholeheartedly look forward to a life of school runs and being the spare part at occasional dinner parties.

As independent and self-sufficient as I have become and as fulfilled as I am, with a rich and varied life, the added dimension of sharing it with someone is, I have to confess, something I occasionally both miss and want.

So, having committed to the idea of committing, if you get my gist, I, like so many other single parents, have had to abide by the apparent rules of single-parent dating. Not least . . .

- Line up your babysitter first. If you haven't got a co-parent to take over then find a trustworthy but cash-strapped teenager with a rudimentary knowledge of first aid and video recorders. Doing this means you're serious about getting out on some dates.

- Stop fibbing. 'My life's perfect just as it is, a partner would simply be the icing on the cake,' has to go. Along with 'I'm sure life is much easier on my own,' and 'I've tried, I just can't seem to meet anyone.'

- Be open to the possibilities. Which, put another way, means look for your opportunities and don't rule anything out, even blind dates and answering, or placing, ads. Believe me, it's worked for a lot of people. I just haven't had the courage of my convictions yet.

- Your children's needs come first. Which means go slowly, don't bring anyone home until you've got to know them, don't introduce them to your child until you've got to know them even better and don't move them in until you know them inside out and back to front.

'I split up with my daughter's father when I was pregnant, after eleven years together. I guess he just didn't like the idea of being a father. I was still in shock when she was born, but I loved her instantly and coping just took over. I was on my own with her until she was seven, when I decided I had to do something about meeting someone new or I'd be waving her off to college on my own and end up as one of those little old ladies taking endless cruises alone. My daughter and I had grown incredibly close and I was worried about bringing someone else in. Would she accept him? Would I? But first I had to meet him.

'I'd had a few dates over the years, but none that had come to anything and it was always hard to meet people. So this time I put an ad in a magazine. I got lots of answers and most of them sounded like perfectly normal, nice people. But when it came to dating them I was terrified. I went for one who'd sent his photo, so I'd at least know who to look for. He was charming, but I was so nervous that I gulped my wine and had to rush into the loo at the wine bar and throw up.

'The next man I saw was obviously a Casanova on the make. He couldn't have been less interested in who I was; he was only interested in getting me into bed. No thanks, I got through that gullible stage at eighteen and I didn't plan to go back there.

'The third guy was nice. Interested and interesting, not

pushy, had a small daughter of his own and appeared relatively unscarred by his divorce. So we dated. For a couple of months we met two or three times a week and I really enjoyed it. Films, meals, walks, he brought me books, made me laugh and took me to nice places.

'Eventually I invited him round for a meal and he met my daughter. I'd already talked to her, lots, about the fact that I would one day meet someone who'd be kind, loving and come to live with us. She'd worked out what criteria were really important: did he like baked beans, did he want a dog and did he like playing games? Luckily he passed on all three counts.

'We married a year later and had a son a year after that. Five years on we're really happy together. We've had plenty of ups and downs, both our girls took a while to get used to the situation, and each other, but they have and now I don't think any one of us would change things. Dating? Go for it!'

Claudia, forty-one, mother of Leah, twelve, and Sam, three

'One of the hardest things is to work out the ideal moment to confess to having children. These days I feel as though "mother" is tattooed in neon letters across my forehead, but as this isn't actually the case, how do you select the ideal moment for mentioning your offspring? Early on, is what I've learned. Drop it into the conversation somewhere between "hello" and "my name is", or at least not far behind. That way those men who are going to run a mile can do so before I've wasted any more time getting to know them.

'The truth is that those who mind you having children don't matter, and those who matter don't mind. I am proud to have my children and I wouldn't want to be with anyone who didn't, once he's adapted to their quirky little ways, feel the same.'

Sue, thirty-three, mother of Tom, six, and Ben, four

'When my husband and I separated and I was left with custody of our two children I thought I was effectively taking a vow of chastity. For quite a long time I would only go on dates when the children were away with their father, but that was okay as I was recovering from the breakdown of my marriage and wasn't looking for another commitment. Today I am seeing someone and we've got to the stage where he stays the night. The children cope with it remarkably well. We kept it a secret for a long time and when he did finally start to stay he would leave at five to seven before the children were woken up at seven. One day they rumbled him and asked if he'd been here overnight. When he said that he had they told him sleepovers were fun! They were very untraumatised and perfectly okay, which surprised me. I expected it to be harder than it was.

'The only advice I could give anyone in a similar position is not to cling to a new man and not to force your children upon them. But do get out there and start dating, it really isn't so difficult.'

Lucy, thirty-nine, mother of Henry, ten and Oliver, eight

'Becoming involved with someone again has sometimes been a quite overwhelming emotional experience, not least due to my son and his myriad of needs which have to run alongside my own and my partner's.

'Making the decision to involve my son very slowly in my new relationship was an enormous step to take, and one that I still question almost daily. It was, however, one I had to take, or give up the possibility of developing a loving, stable relationship with another adult.

'As the relationship progresses so does the stark realisation that the days of youthful freedom are gone for ever. Dating as I recall it is a thing of the past. Now that I have a child there's an entirely different set of rules. Spontaneity has been redefined because when there's a child to take care of plans have to be made. Nowadays practicalities and responsibilities come first, but at the same time it's been vital to make time for me and my new partner. Apart from anything else, a happy, relaxed parent breeds a happy, relaxed child.'

Pam, thirty-nine, mother of Jake, seven

So there you have it. It can be done, and there are plenty of happy couples around to prove it. And for those of us still out there, still raking up the nerve and the energy to fix that grin in place and go out there yet again, hope lives on. As for infallible advice, I'm afraid there is none. Logical when you think about it. If I were that successful at this little pastime I'd have called a halt to it long ago and be happily married by now. Rest assured, I'm not out there dating for fun. Perhaps it's just me and I'm missing the point, but this isn't an opportunity I embrace with open arms. If pain is the touchstone of growth I'd prefer to remain stunted on this one.

A new addition . . .

The quest for the perfect partner to join you and your offspring is not encouraged, of course, by statistics. Apparently the more you marry the more likely you are to get divorced and second marriages are twice as likely to break up as first-timers. Or so Relate comfortingly offers. Hmm. How encouraging. At this point I'm tempted to lie down and die, but no time for that, there's a school run to do. And the fact remains that it's great to have someone else deal with the occasional crisis and who'll tell you it's okay, even if it's a lie you don't believe for a split second.

So while I know where Gloria Steinem was coming from when she said, 'A woman without a man is like a fish without a bicycle', I have to confess to still hoping and wishing that one day my life will be permanently full with three instead of two. And while I'm on the subject, if any of my friends who tell me men must be queuing at my door could let them know they've got the wrong address, I'd be so grateful.

But, for those who are a few steps further along the path to happy-ever-after coupledom than I am, what happens when the big moment comes? When the new man in your life is ready to move in and you're ready to let him. Here you are, full of optimism and heady plans, shoving your jumpers aside to make room for his shirts and boxer shorts and convinced that sharing your space and your life, while not easy, is infinitely worth it. But how do you break it to the kids? How do you ease him in and re-shape family life to include him, with minimum interference to your offspring's lives and routines?

'It's a big upheaval for everyone, and there's no way round that. I'd been on my own with two children for five years when I met Mark. The kids liked him from the start, but they were still outraged when, a year later, I said he was moving in. The six-year-old lay on the floor screaming, "Make him go away." What did we do? Try to comfort and reassure him, pour ourselves a stiff drink and accept that it might be a bumpy ride. In fact things settled down very fast, once the kids realised that this was the way it was going to be. Mark and I made sure that we didn't argue in front of them and that we backed each other up, so that the kids never saw an opening to come between us. Mark made sure he spent time with each of them alone, doing things they enjoyed. And apart from that we just got on with life and dealt with problems as they arose.

'It's been three years now and we're all still going strong.'

Rachel, thirty-eight, mother of Rebecca, nine, and Joe, seven

'The first single parent I got involved with had an amazingly strong bond with her child and adopted the unspoken attitude of "This is my baby and no one is coming between us." She indulged his every whim and dedicated all her time to him, with the result that when Sam came to adolescent rebellion time he did it in spades.

'If a couple are together when a baby comes along it's

generally the husband's nose that gets put out of joint. As a single parent, when you get involved with someone it's the child's nose which is put out. When Sam was little I was clearly the competition for his mother's affection and, after basking in it 100 per cent himself, I was not always welcomed and he kicked up a stink.

'If I'd been a younger man I think I'd have found this quite difficult, but as it was I had a child of my own already, so it was less of an issue that there wasn't much time left over for me.

'Sam's mother and I were a couple for eight years but we never lived together, mainly because of him. He was so disruptive that she wouldn't take the risk.

'Would I do it again? I did! The chances are that once you're past a certain age you have to, if you want to be with someone of a similar age.

'I now live with my new partner, whose daughter lives with us. My son, who's now twenty-one, visits us regularly. Things are more straightforward this time around, because my partner involved me in her life and her daughter accepted me much more easily.

'My advice to a single mum who's beginning to date? Put your partner before your child from time to time, even if just occasionally – otherwise our delicate male egos get ever so slightly dented!'

Adam, fifty, father of Tom, twenty-one

'When my new partner moved in with us I thought we'd done everything perfectly. My daughter behaved beautifully and seemed to welcome him, she liked it when he put her to bed and cuddled up with him in front of the

TV. I was doing handstands. But after a week she asked me when he was going home. And when I said he wasn't, that this was his home now, she burst into tears. I felt terrible, I'd thought that she understood, but she didn't really. She was only five and it had always been just her and me.

'It took a lot longer before she really accepted him. We never pushed it or tried to force her to do things with him. And I gave her lots of cuddles and reassurance about how much I loved her every day. Now, a couple of years down the line, I can see how genuinely close to him she is. Last Father's Day she drew him a lovely card and it meant a lot to him. He's been very patient and has stuck in there, doing his share of looking after her, even when she was rejecting him. I saw tears in his eyes when he got the card and I realised how hard it's been for him, often feeling on the outside because I was so close to her. It takes determination and sticking power to create a successful stepfamily.'

Gail, thirty-five, mother of Josie, seven

As with dating, there's no real right and wrong, only the best you can do at the time. Making your children's wellbeing a priority doesn't mean always giving in to them. In fact a child who can drive away your new partner is often scared by having that much power. Kids need to know who's in charge, and that it's not them. They can accept that you love another adult, as long as they're always given plenty of love, security and honesty. Honest!

Wipe wisdom

- Once your child is catered for, never feel bad about having your own needs met.

- Develop a rapid filtering process for prospective dates. I tend to draw the line, for example, at being set up on a blind date with a man who'd had a hip replacement, on the basis that I was about to have one myself and a friend thought we would have a lot in common. It transpired, not surprisingly, that the ability to set off a metal detector was not enough to bring us together.

- At dinner parties, when asked 'What do you do?' avoid replying 'I'm a mother.' It's all too often met with an almost immediate back view of the interrogator's head. 'The best I can,' generally commands a little more respect and interest and has even been known to lead to conversation, if not quite a second date.

7

New World Order

Hide away your valuables – Shortie's on the loose

However much you might have thought you had a grip on life in those blissfully ignorant pre-children days, as a parent you're plunged headlong into a series of new situations and unexpected demands which make you re-think the whole concept of getting a grip. In fact I'm not entirely convinced that it's possible to feel anything other than a little alien in this strange new world of small folk. The world order as we knew and, with hindsight, loved it, disappears, to be replaced by world chaos on an alarming scale. And the next few years are mostly going to be spent trying to make some sense and order out of the chaos, and generally failing miserably.

Your home, no matter how pristine it once was, will now be reduced to a rubble of plastic toys, bottles and beakers and trails of small items of clothing. Things will be lost or broken on a regular basis. You'll trail around the house in a futile search for the TV remote control, your other shoe or your favourite earrings, some of which will turn up three weeks later and the rest of which will turn up next time you move house.

Time, that once reliable measure of your ability to function on a normal basis, will become one of your greatest puzzles – and challenges. How can it take three hours to feed and change a baby and then get yourself dressed? Is it possible to get yourself plus small child out of the front door in reasonable order in under half a day? No greater challenge is known to woman – or man.

And then there's your social life. Where once you made intelligent conversation at dinner parties, now you simply grin inanely and discuss the price of nappies at parent and baby groups, or shriek yourself hoarse trying to explain 'pin the tail on the donkey' to a bunch of five-year-olds at children's parties. Lovely!

Damage limitation

In pre-parenting days I thought having a child meant raising another life. How naïve could one woman be? I failed to understand that it also meant raising everything in my life, at least two feet higher if anything was to survive.

New baby home from hospital, I surveyed the happy scene, blissfully unaware of the degree of imminent devastation lying patiently in wait. My main concern in the early days was to ensure my son didn't roll off the changing table, but to be honest he wasn't about to roll anywhere for quite some time. In fact I was beginning to get quite bored until one afternoon I turned around for a moment, turned back and he was gone! Finally, I had a 'roller'.

Along with the pride came the need, from that day on,

to be one step ahead and anticipate his every move. How I even began to think that was possible is beyond me. I'm rarely sure what I'm going to do next, much less him. From here on in I lived in a world that necessitated seeing everything from the eye and hand level of a two-foot-tall dynamo, which meant that the entire contents of our lives had to be raised three feet from the ground. I'd like to have seen the *Changing Rooms* team make our place look normal.

How can small children learn such amazing developmental concepts as speech but take so long to grasp the simple fact that sticking sucked, wet fingers in an electrical socket is not a great start to anybody's day, least of all their own? Another child and to hell with the mobile, I'm hanging up a simple list of dos and don'ts.

- Don't go near the cooker.
- Don't touch the pretty orange flame.
- Don't grab handles.
- Don't pull tablecloths.
- Leave my caffeine alone – it's hot and it's mine.
- Don't drink white spirit stored in lemonade bottles. Strange for any grown-up to pass their time decanting chemicals, but rest assured we'll never cease to amaze you.
- Don't expect pressed clothes – ironing's out of the question now.
- Don't stick your head in the washing machine – the rest of your body just might follow.
- Don't even look like you want to be left alone in the bath.

- Don't go up the stairs when we forget to close the gates.
- Don't pull on electrical flexes, however long and with whatever promise of unknown appliances at their end.
- Don't pick up Daddy's cigarettes and especially not his lighter and matches.
- Forget the longing looks at the fireguard.
- Don't go near the window, particularly not with that chair.
- And, while I am at it, stop swinging on the curtain ropes.

In short, I learned that the vaguely aesthetically pleasing place I had once called home was now a war and combat zone. War because every sharp corner, lacking an attractive spongy thing, and in fact every other item we owned spelled danger and potential disaster – and combat because from here on in we were locked in it. My life became entirely devoted to saying 'No!' Explanations were useless. 'No!' was all that was required of me. On reflection I could quite easily have run a looping tape with my 'calm, but consistently firm' voice droning on all day. No one would have been any the wiser, or paid any more attention. My son resembled a small but unstoppable dinosaur, bandy legs manoeuvring him from one potential mishap to another. I just wish the *Krypton Factor* was still on air. Games such as completing simple chores while keeping a small child happy, safe and amused are no mean feat.

His world became my world and from now on he wasn't safe to be left, even for a moment. Not that I could have left him, even if I wanted to. From the moment he was on his feet it was obvious that I was never going to get a moment's peace from here on in, as Shortie decided to make it his life's mission to follow me everywhere. Even the loo offered no remission, it was just as much his as mine these days. I had a full-time shadow, just not quite the same size as my body. I'd like to offer some words of comfort at this point but I'm afraid I can't. In fact, once you've sorted out the inside and got used to your new, permanently attached child-size accessory, there are still plenty more unmitigated disasters to come, in the form of the outside world.

First, there's the garden to contend with – an absolute delight of hidden horrors. I thought I'd avoided this one, as we had no garden, but junior wasn't about to let me off that lightly and for the next few months my time was consumed with preventing my son from launching himself off the window box. But if I felt sorry for myself I felt worse for my parents, as buckets were emptied, ponds drained or covered up and garden chemicals locked away. Take heart, though. Once you've ripped up all the poisonous plants, regardless of how long it's taken to cultivate them in the first place, once the children have survived, grown up and left home, you'll have all the time in the world to try to recreate what you had so lovingly grown in the first place. That is until the grandchildren come along.

And now you can take back that sigh of relief; it doesn't stop here. Once you've childproofed your own home, you can go out and have a nervous breakdown in other people's.

'Children arrived and I had to put my record collection away. That and selling the car were the biggest nightmares about the whole thing! Alongside minor irritants like elastic bands on kitchen cupboard doors, having to have a loft extension to accommodate the unexpected third arrival, painting the entire house in a high-gloss wipeable finish and turning my office into a playroom – nothing much has changed.'

Jack, forty-four, father of Christopher, seven, Alex, five, and Meg, two

'Our daughter is only five months old, so we haven't had to face childproofing our home yet, although I do envisage us having to move to somewhere completely padded in the not too distant future. If not financially possible a playpen, permanently, will have to be the solution.'

Rachel, thirty, mother of Maia, five months

'I was determined to change nothing about our home when our son arrived until the time when we were sitting in our bedroom admiring how advanced he was, sitting up beautifully at only five months. As the words came from our mouths we watched in horror as he fell backwards on to the polished wooden floorboards. Crack, and off to Accident and Emergency to check for concussion. After that everything was padded, raised or simply stored until a later date. From one extreme to the other pretty much sums it up! The best safety items we've acquired have to be the stair gates. Useful to stop my son escaping, useful because if my hips touched the sides I knew I'd put on too much weight, and useful when they refuse to open should I ever want a career as a champion hurdler once motherhood's over and done with.'

Sheila, thirty-two, mother of Georgie, one

'I made a decision when we had kids that I wasn't going to change anything in our home. I'm glad I did really, because when they came along and got a little older they caused chaos and I realised then that if I had started to raise things up and put things away that we'd have had nothing left of ours at all for a long, long time. I would have had to remove my whole life! The only thing I did do was put safety gates everywhere and cushions in front of the patio doors to stop them falling out of the kitchen, down the steps and into the garden. That was a must.'

Robina, thirty-eight, mother of Dina, seven, and Zara, four

'There were gates everywhere, plug covers over every socket, and the kitchen was rearranged so all breakables were at the top. The problem is that I have never had time to change it back and now you have easy access to one heck of a lot of Tupperware and everything else no longer makes any sense. The other thing we had to resort to was a bigger bed, resulting in a much smaller bedroom. But it soon became clear that he was never going to leave us alone for a minute so we caved in, reckoning that if we were going to be permanently sleepless we might at least be comfortable.'

Jo, forty-one, mother of Sasha, five

'I can only tell you that with three small children our home was ruined. There were gates put in everywhere that ruined the wood, I never quite got around to putting a throw over the settee so that got ruined too, and then to send me completely insane as I sat amongst the rubble I could only open the windows two inches even on boiling hot summer days. The only thing I drew the line at was putting a lock on my bedroom door – but boy was I tempted and often still am!'

Claire, forty-five, mother of Damian, ten, Finn, eight, and Cameron, two

In conclusion I can only say that, as you prepare your home for assault on every front and put into storage anything you've ever really valued, you can comfort yourself with the reminder that they are, after all, only possessions, and it's perhaps not worth shedding a tear for something that couldn't cry for you.

Church hall hell

Team player? Not me, I'm afraid. I was never keen on that aspect of life at school, preferring to have an eclectic group of friends and somewhat lacking in the gang mentality. I couldn't even summon up much commitment to the games teams, opting for tennis every time as then at least you only had yourself to answer to. And apparently not much has changed now I've supposedly arrived in full-blown adulthood, and parenthood to boot. The prospect of joining the antenatal class when pregnant was horrifying enough and, if I remember correctly, I only made it to the Question and Answer session, carefully and rather successfully avoiding all gatherings to discuss contractions, breathing, breast-feeding and other such matters. Following childbirth the opportunity to join a plethora of other mother and baby groups frankly filled me with dread and loathing.

I know mother and baby groups work for a lot of people, and there are no doubt loads of exceptional ones all over the country, but they didn't work for me. I felt an all-consuming compulsion to avoid damp church halls packed out with parents and small offspring, busy learning the delights of banging drums, shaking tambourines and blowing vigorously into wind instruments and to steer clear of sincere talks over herbal tea with women wearing Birkenstocks. After all, why should wearing a dried-out old piece of leather, closely resembling an Italian delicatessen's home-cured meat counter, attached to one's feet, hold any appeal? Instead I opted for finding one or two mothers, through luck more than judgement, whom I really connected with.

It worked for me, but didn't assuage the guilt that, although I knew beyond a doubt that I would go insane in a mother and toddler group, I was in some way damaging my child's ability to socialise and develop as normal. Once a guilty parent, always a guilty parent. Compensation lay in the knowledge that my new friends were parents who could share how they felt. Their fears, their anxieties, their joys, and roar with laughter too. It was, and still is, an uplifting experience for me to have these friendships in my life, and the friendships they have brought my son too. The pay-off has to be more worth while than the guilt and the day that stops I'll join the church hall brigade.

The other price I paid was a certain amount of time,

in fact a considerable amount of time, at home alone with my child, and Home Alone comes at a price you have to be willing to pay. For me, seeing my friends as and when we could and spending the time with my son was enough. I'd be lying, however, if I claimed that I was happy 24/7. There were moments, and even longer periods than that, of loneliness and isolation. But despite that, it worked best for us.

Groups just aren't my cup of tea, herbal or otherwise, and frankly since having my son I've needed coffee and a lot of it. I'm sure I remember hearing that behind every great man is an even greater woman, or words to that effect. Today I'm convinced that behind every great woman is a great deal of caffeine. So the occasional bout of isolation and the feelings that brought with it was a price I became willing to pay.

> 'I had a year off after my daughter was born, so we trotted along to the local mother and baby group, which I was convinced would be pointless and boring. How wrong I was! I met a really nice bunch of women, some of them neighbours of mine I'd never got around to meeting because of the long hours I worked pre-baby. It was nice to sit and talk, swap information and get answers to my endless baby questions from mothers who'd done it all before. My daughter loved it too; she could crawl around having dribbling contests with the other babies, while we mothers downed gallons of tea and bonded over our nappy bags. Corny as it all was, I really enjoyed it and I'm still good friends with several of the women I met there.'
>
> *Sally, thirty-four, mother of Harriet, three*

'I went to a mother and baby group and loathed it. Every child was with a nanny, so I spent two hours surrounded by small kids being looked after by slightly older ones, felt isolated and consequently never went back. I had been to antenatal groups to see if I could learn anything about avoiding unnecessary pain, and how to bath the baby, but I didn't make any lasting friendships there, and the mother and baby group was the same. Perhaps it's me but I seem to have the same friends that I had before having children, and that suits us fine. I only went back to the antenatal groups for each subsequent birth in the vain hope that something had changed, like less pain and more drugs!'

Jemima, twenty-nine, mother of Emma, six, Claire, three, and Jason, six months

'I actually ended up running our local mother and baby group, when someone else dropped out. Six or seven mums with various offspring in tow would pitch up once a week and compare ordeals of the mine-was-up-all-night-and-vomited-fifteen-times variety, over tea and biscuits. What was nice about it was realising that I wasn't alone in the moments when I doubted motherhood was for me. We'd laugh about the awful bits and it always really cheered me up. We also provided a support system for each other. More than once I phoned one of the others in the middle of the night when I wasn't sure whether to call a doctor or not.'

Ruth, thirty-one, mother of Cameron, five, and Daisy, three

'Oh, yes, I went. I had to make myself do it though and can honestly say I didn't enjoy it one little bit. Does anyone really? The worst had to be the baby groups when no one wanted to be the first to take their baby off the breast and on to the bottle and when they did they'd justify it by saying, "Of course he's growing so fast he needed that little bit more." The truth for me is that I was just fed up with breast-feeding.

'I couldn't stand the mother and baby music groups either, and the prospect of going again after just one visit was simply too much. Coffee mornings weren't much better. I was so consumed with envy in the end I had to stop going. Sitting around and saying, "You look so well," when what I wanted to scream was "Bitch!" as I envied their flatter stomachs was just too much for me.'

Kirsty, thirty-three, mother of Liam, three

A whole new theme

Hmm. The opportunity for public displays of unmanageability. What more could a parent ask for? And on top of that, the chance to be around hundreds of other children as well as just your own! Yes, it's time for an outing. Oh, goody. And the possibilities of where to go are endless. It's just unfortunate that Harvey Nichols for a spot of retail therapy and a long and leisurely lunch just aren't my child's idea of a fun way to pass the time. Perhaps it's my own fault and I should have trained him better. Or perhaps it's just part of parenthood that we have to learn to do the things they want to do. Compromise I think it's called. When you don't get what you want, as my son more succinctly puts it. So what exciting little trips shall we plan this year? And how, as a reasonably balanced thirty-four-year-old, am I going to adjust to this new world of Technicolor nightmares?

From Disneyland to theme parks, and even just the local park, all, I'm afraid, fill me with horror. Theme parks, especially. I'd rate boiling my head higher on a list of preferred activities than opting for a day out at one of these. They bring out the worst in everyone. I tell my son we're only going once or twice a year as these places are very expensive and therefore a huge treat. But let's be honest, that's only part of the truth. The rest lies in the fact that the more frequent the trips, the more likely I am to tip over the edge of sanity into the darkness beyond. Madness is in the next-door room, a friend wisely told me, and after our first theme-park experience I've never doubted him for a minute.

'You know people who've been to theme parks, and you're fully aware of just how long the wide-eyed, vacant, somewhere-else look lasts. You know it's going to be bad. Really bad. But exactly how bad is, like childbirth, impossible to say until you do it. And you know you have to do it. Because somewhere around three days after their sixth birthday children appear to develop an innate knowledge about the existence of such places. So despite the knowledge you have of such horrors, unless you belong to the Cruella de Ville school of parenting you have to take them – at least once.

'There is something intrinsically pleasing to kids about seeing determinedly grinning, middle-aged adults being flung from here to eternity in a giant steel cage. And worth more than a passing snigger is the sight of me being outstandingly crap at the shooting range – just like they knew, and said, I would be. And if the Jaws of Death ride doesn't leave you queasy, the prices certainly will. Even something long and squishy in a roll and a mouthful of tooth-rotting fizz in a paper cup will test already battered purses. At the entry gate paying for a family of four means you can easily kiss goodbye to the equivalent of at least two bottles of Christian Dior nail polish, a new pair of shoes and a fair few Häagen-Dazs.

'And there's more. A curious thing about the customers theme parks attract is that an unreasonable number of them are wasps. When they aren't scaring children with sticky red lollies, they are busy dive-bombing the log flume, winding beadily through queues of sweaty adolescents and stinging any portion of bare flesh they can aim their rumps at. But the point is that your kids will love the playground kudos that a visit to a theme park brings. They'll brag themselves silly about how they weren't scared at all, how the rides were all rather tame really, and that although they didn't quite get on the most petrifying ride – because the queues were so long, of course – they went on the biggest log flume in Europe nine times. They'll develop selective memory and a fierce addiction to thrills which will last into adulthood, enabling them to forget that they got so wet that they shivered, that they got so tired that they cried, that the candy floss made them nauseous, and that they spent more time waiting in line than they did on any ride. Like any addiction, they'll want their fix again and again.

'Be afraid, be VERY afraid.'

With grateful thanks to Jane Cunningham. Reproduced from WIPE *magazine*

'Theme parks – can't bear them, and it doesn't help that I'm terrified of heights. Even standing on the kitchen table is too much for me. We have caved in though and have done Disney which was great. Mainly because my mum came and she did all the scary stuff whilst I stuck to on-the-ground things! The memories are great.'

Robina, thirty-eight, mother of Dina, seven, and Zara, four

'We took our kids to Disneyland, Paris and I can only conclude that it is bizarre how we come to appreciate theme parks. We went with a child who was disabled and as a result got immediate access to every ride, so I can't recommend that one enough. Disney has to be the tension capital of the universe, over-tall, synthetic creatures, relentlessly happy staff and retail opportunities at every turn. It costs so much and you HAVE to have a good time. They plan it so that you are somehow supposed to like it in a particular way – one ride on each adventure and then watch the parade, but children being children want to do the same ride fifty times and it's always Space Mountain. There's such a conflict between their vision and how children really respond.

'The one purpose it did serve was to tell us what stage our children were at. Our five-year-old loved it – pliable but with tantrums along the way. My husband's twelve- and fifteen-year-olds, however, were a different story. From ten onwards they appear to become independent and from twelve onwards they hate you. It was very hard. We spent every penny we had and more on taking them. All that had changed was now they got to hate us in Disney.'

Maggie, forty-two, mother of Josh, five

> 'Museums are just about all I can cope with when it comes to outings with my children. That way we all have a vaguely good time, once you've dealt with the tantrums and everything else that goes hand in hand with taking your small children anywhere. Other than that I can only do places that have a lot of greenery and don't involve a large number of children in an enclosed space. Theme parks have to be the worst and I quite simply refuse to go. Just the very thought of them conjures up horrific images in my mind of plastic and ugly things and I can feel my soul beginning to decay in front of my eyes. They never go and as a result when my children do get taken anywhere with even a simple bouncy castle, they are the noisiest and wildest children there. No doubt because they are so clearly deprived!'
>
> *Laura, thirty-four, mother of Sam, three, and Thomas, one*

Get down. Get dirty

Parties. In my recollection they were about having a good time, getting drunk and getting down. Today, since we're all a little older and a lot more exhausted, party appears to equate to a drink and a polite chat. No longer are we in search of quite the same new experiences, new friendships, hot dates and wild fun. I used to arrive home at four in the morning and feel dead for three days. These days someone needs me at six a.m. and two hours' sleep just isn't enough. The wildest parties I get to now are the ones thrown for my small son or by his friends, and frankly they are about as exhausting as I can cope with.

Our first foray into such frolics was, without a doubt, one of the highest ranking stressful experiences since parenthood began. Living in a housing association flat where the walls and floor are made of cardboard, and paper in areas where they ran a bit short, resulted in the necessity of giving our downstairs neighbour a very large voucher for redemption at the local off-licence. While he went to the pub before returning home and swigging his bounty, thereby remaining entirely immune to the goings-on in my flat, I could only stand by, longing to go downstairs and join him. But ensuring everyone had a good time and that my child would be the most popular thing at nursery since sliced bread, for the next day or two at least, was to be my lot.

It's just unfortunate that it came at the somewhat extravagant cost of my hearing. Not to mention the erosion of my sanity and thirty children high on E numbers liberally smearing every piece of furniture in sight with food and cake and generally trashing the place. Not an experience I will be repeating in a hurry. In fact, ever. I've made my stand. From now on hiring a venue and inviting an entertainer is the only way. Let Bobo the clown deal with the madness while I retreat with a cup of tea or something stronger. Apart from anything else I am no longer willing to sit up all night before the appointed date carefully drawing a donkey whose fate is to be repeatedly stabbed with its own tail the next day.

Party entertainers always look slightly creepy in my experience. And why they should choose this particular occupation as a career I find even more sinister. But, let's be fair, they do keep the children relatively under control and give them a good time. Apart from the one little monster who always bursts into tears of terror at the sight of Bobo's inanely grinning face. Creepiness aside, entertainers cost the earth. But if it meant my going without food for a week, or even a month, that's a price I'm quite willing to pay, having tried throwing a party without one.

> 'Always, always do it somewhere other than your own home. If there's one thing I've learned from experience it's that if you have your child's party at home you end up laying on a party for the mums too and on top of that your home gets trashed. So sod the expense, do it somewhere else.'
>
> *Robin, thirty-two, mother of Peter, five*

> 'Mr Will He Won't He? He's the answer to all my prayers. He just pitches up and takes over whenever it's birthday-party time. The only thing I do agree to for each of my sons' birthdays is to hold them at our home. There's something rather nice about it somehow, that gives me an old-fashioned sense of how it should be. But when it comes to actually doing anything more than opening the front door, I hand over to the entertainer.'
>
> *Sue, thirty-nine, mother of Jonathan, seven, Stephen, five, and Edmund, three*

> 'I hate children's parties. They're bloody hard work and an absolute nightmare and why I keep having them at home is beyond me. Every year I say that next time

we're going out. Finally, after years of chaos I've booked McDonald's for my younger daughter's fifth. I tell my eldest two that we're all going out for a family meal together to celebrate as it's more grown-up. They buy that, so everyone's happy!'

Katherine, thirty-seven, mother of Sarah, ten, Rory, eight, and Zoe, four

'When I was six these types of shindings were nearly always the same. There was usually an entertainer. The entertainer usually looked rather like a potential child molester but he did silly tricks, told silly stories and made us laugh. If we were his helpers he'd give us a Spangle and if we were very, very good he'd turn a balloon into a flower. If there were boys at the party they'd snatch the balloon and pretend it was a sword and the child molester would get cross. After musical chairs we'd sit down around a rented trestle table and eat red jelly out of paper bowls, along with crustless egg sandwiches, chocolate fingers, crisps and a Smartie birthday cake. When it was time to go home we'd leave with a bit of cake wrapped up in a piece of kitchen roll and a droopy balloon in need of Viagra.

'Nowadays children's parties are extravaganzas. They're often held in venues – nightmarish locations like the Discovery Zone, Planet Hollywood . . . They're heavily themed, often catered and, worst of all, every child receives a party bag. I am a mother who hates party bags. Putting party bags together is like filling multitudes of mini Christmas stockings for children who aren't yours. And they're potentially just as expensive. My daughter recently attended a party which was held at the Durley House Hotel. I slung a Beanie Baby into some recycled wrapping paper, silently commending myself on finding an obscure critter and was appalled when she returned with her "Party Favour" which was three limited-edition Beanies, custom-wrapped in showy-off Cellophane. I'm forty years old and have never been to the Durley House Hotel, much less been given a gift for pitching up, and frankly I'm cheesed off.

'To receive a present just for being at a party is topsy-turvy, and has the undesired effect of turning small children into rabid socialites. Kids are innately avaricious and obligatory party bags have sent them into overdrive, causing them to accept invitations from children they actively dislike in order not to miss out on the treats. It's all too over the top and almost belittles the child whose birthday it actually is. The back seat of my car is living testimony to the pointlessness of party bags, for the contents lie in post-party disappointment on the floor and in the cracks between the seats.

'I'm all for having children have the best time of their lives, but they have to grow up recognising the difference between a present and a party bag. A present is something you give to someone you like. A party bag is extremely expensive and preferably made by Lulu Guinness.'

With grateful thanks to Sarah Standing. Reproduced from WIPE *magazine*

Wipe wisdom

- Develop the power of lateral thinking.

- Never mind about locking away your daughters, just lock away your knives, scissors, razors, sewing kits, buttons, beads, coins, hard objects, soft objects, hard and soft objects with detachable bits, big things, small things, big parts, small parts . . .

- Compromise, but carefully, and only occasionally.

- When giving parties for people under three feet tall cater immediately for every possible eventuality from the more obvious to the downright bizarre and obscure.

- And remember, whatever you do, don't sell your soul. Stick to what you enjoy. As Rita Mae Brown so wisely said: 'Almost all you can do in life is be who you are. Some people will love you for you. Most will love you for what you can do for them, and some won't love you at all.'

8

Toddler Terrorists

Discipline – who's really in charge?

The terrible twos. It's more than a little wipe lie, it's a downright fib. Such a seemingly innocent phrase led me to believe that guerrilla warfare and the tactics necessary to stay one step ahead, survive and perhaps even retain an ounce of sanity, would all pretty much be done with once this delightful little phase had been played out. The truth? The truth is that from there you're plunged straight into the terrifying threes, the fearsome fours . . . the list goes on, and, unfortunately, on. Once your little one has discovered he has a separate entity and a will of his own, all hell appears to break loose. Generally at high volume and, almost without exception, in a public place.

What I'd most like to know is how they manage it? How do such little people, undeveloped in so many ways, have such sophisticated mechanisms for winding us up? Every button that can possibly be pressed is pressed. How do they do that? Insider information? Were they simply cramming up while lurking in the womb? 'Hmm, nothing better to do for nine months except get to grips with grown-ups' foibles and hang-ups and tap into anything else I can possibly use against them at a later date. That should pass the time nicely.'

Just how did our innocent, blameless small babies grow into such toddler terrorists and how do even the most saintly among us survive the onslaught?

Repeat after me: this is normal

When I was pregnant I had such high hopes for my standards of discipline. I'd always be the one in control, be firm, calm and consistent in my approach and I would never raise my voice, much less my hand, to my child. Today I have to confess to failing consistently at the former and having smacked on two occasions, neatly failing at the latter too. My belief that I would always know instinctively how to respond and never overreact just didn't allow for how I would feel when reality and exhaustion struck. At moments like these calm consistency proved just a little beyond my reach. As a result I've found myself wondering on many an occasion whether I am the wrong kind of parent or whether I simply have the wrong kind of child.

Most parenting books advise us that our children will go through a variety of developmental experiences and milestones. They'll sit around six months and walk around twelve. And who among us can honestly say that they didn't feel that slightest twinge of parental paranoia if their child was a month or two slower than their contemporaries? But the one milestone I suspect few of us are in any hurry to reach is the onslaught of the terrible twos. Those long and blissful days when your child insists on hurling itself repeatedly against every boundary in sight. But apparently, so the experts say, this is a good thing. Our little treasures need to explode, to bite, to hit, to tell whoppers, and generally to learn that they are separate beings in order to distinguish the acceptable from the unacceptable. Why can't they just ask us?

Alongside all this, hopefully they also begin to develop some self-control, to test out their sense of independence and their capabilities before unfortunately then needing to express their extreme frustration at being stopped or not quite capable of achieving the goal in hand. And I thought it was just a tantrum.

> 'How does a baby become a toddler? What process is it that transforms that soft little bundle of joy, or bundle of something soft at any rate, into a terrorist in a sleepsuit?
>
> 'One minute they're hairless, helpless and bereft of guile. The next they're ordering pizzas on your credit card and banging out the message on their cot bars that in the toddler-dominated, ice cream-on-demand, market economy of the future, there'll be no room for dinosaurs like you, Daddio.
>
> 'What accounts for this metamorphosis? How can anyone acquire such streetwise savvy after just a couple of trips to the Early Learning Centre? Surely it can't be merely graduating to solids? Let's face it, anyone else who tried to get all bolshy while wearing a nappy would risk contempt and ridicule, but toddlers get away with it.

'And the key to toddle control – their control of us rather than our control of them – lies back in babyhood. According to the experts the infant brain develops at a phenomenal rate, which cannot be sustained. Otherwise, by the time we made it to puberty, we'd all be contemplating black holes in space rather than the blackheads on face.

'This is something adults, whose brains have already gone into steep and irreversible decline, seldom appreciate until it's too late. They think Hey, what can this kid possibly know? He's just a baby. I'm the smart one around here. I MADE the baby, I call the shots.

'Suckers. Why don't they get this? During that first year when babies appear to have nothing on their minds at all except remembering to suck, burp, wail and excrete – they're actually making plans. They lie there in their cots – looking up at dumb faces, making stupid goo-goo gah-gah noises – and they think, These adults really aren't much of an advance up on the evolutionary ladder. Just wait till I can toddle – I'll soon have them eating these god-awful baby dinners they keep giving me out of the palm of my hand.

'Of course they don't SAY this. They keep their cards closer to their chests than vapour rub. But all the time they're accumulating new brain cells at the same astronomical rate that you and I are losing them. You won't be aware of it at the time, but all the marbles in the house are gradually being transferred. Until, one day, as the old Roy Orbison song goes "Your baby's not your baby any more." You've got the toddler instead.

'In marsupial terms this is the point where junior climbs

out of the pouch. In human ones it's where you should prepare to go out of your mind. Because what may have been the slight pitfalls of running your own baby successfully become yawning chasms when you graduate into toddler management.

'Feeding time for example. A bland diet of milk and mush will no longer suffice. Now you have to tickle their jaded palates with interesting tit-bits in intriguing shapes for them to hurl on the floor or smear over the nearest available surface.

'I wish I had picked up some of my daughter's in-your-face style of culinary criticism in the days when I was still free to eat out. Not for her the hesitant "not-worth-making-a-fuss" approach when things aren't up to scratch. No. If you don't like what's on your plate, don't just sit there. Spit it out. Maybe even writhe around a bit as if you've just been poisoned. That way, Dad, the dumb waiter always gets the message.

'Another cute trick, kids, if you're not feeling very hungry, is to get the old man so concerned that you should eat the dinner he's made that he'll convince himself your plastic spoon has somehow become a railway locomotive. He even does the noises like he's really loco, and the commentary: "Chuff, chuff, train coming out of the station – heading for the tunnel, chuff, chuff, chuff, whoo, whoo."

'The first time this happens your mouth/railway tunnel will be open, with astonishment, and he'll manage to get the spoon/5.15 from Crewe into it before you realise. After that though, just remember to keep it shut, and you'll be able to watch Pop really lose it. I've had more rail cancellations than hot dinners since becoming a parent.

'But if getting food in at the front is hard, cleaning up at the back is no holiday either. The weirdest thing about the toddler metabolism is that the amount of material they import up top bears little, or no, relation to the amount of stuff they can export down below. My own toddler has perfected the art of moving mountains without any apparent intake. She can sit in her highchair through any number of abortive mealtimes as if her jaws have been wired. You'd swear she's not eating enough to keep a sparrow alive, and yet, when it comes to changing her nappy, it's as if the eagle has landed. How one baked bean and half a fish finger can generate such a heap is one of life's great unsolved toddler mysteries.

'Something else which marks the transition of baby to toddler is the fact that baby poo is predictable and babies tend to stay fixed to the spot while having their bottoms wiped. But there is no such in situ certainty with a toddler. Somehow having a full nappy is an aid rather than a handicap to a toddler's agility and the smell that wafts in their wake seems only to heighten their determination not to be pinned to the changing mat. So first you must capture then cajole.

'Diversionary tactics are once again called for, and it's here I find a unicycle comes in handy. It gives both speed and manoeuvrability in pursuit and is a distraction once you have run your quarry to the ground. Other ways of diverting their attention include card tricks and yodelling. You could even try developing your own range of amusing facial ticks to distract them, as you sing – in the style of Pavarotti – the theme from *Postman Pat*.

'If all this fails, prepare to wrestle. But be warned: bottom wiping a moving target is not for the squeamish.

'But perhaps the biggest single hurdle to be surmounted each day is the bedtime ritual. Climbing the little wooden hill to Bedfordshire can seem like climbing Everest the hard way. The very mention of the words "bed" or "sleep" – so welcoming and luxurious to knackered parents – are my little girl's clarion call to mutiny. You may just have been having a lovely time together playing with teddy and having lots of hugs but just one hint that you're about to break out the pyjamas, and Beirut breaks out instead.

'It was all so different when I was a kid. On the *Magic Roundabout* when Zebedee used to say "Time for bed", his word was law. You didn't get any backchat from Dougal or Florence throwing a wobbly. Somehow, though, my words carry less authority than those of a moustached wooden puppet mounted on a spring. And that can be a mite depressing.'

With grateful thanks to Mark Whitaker, radio presenter and writer.

Reproduced from WIPE *magazine*

In the line of fire

My own experience was a little different from the norm although I'm sure I'm far from alone in this. The terrible twos never quite happened, or certainly not on cue. Why? I suspect because my son was ill throughout those early years and with numerous operations, hospital stays and bouts of medication, he was hardly ready to start testing any boundaries. When he reached the grand old age of five I sighed with relief. Not only was he getting healthier and stronger but we had escaped the two-year-old tantrums. But there followed what can only be described as a rude awakening.

Uninvited, the devil himself took up permanent residence in our house. My son still physically resembled his former self but some days I wouldn't have batted an eyelid if his head had started to spin. For a while it can only be described as *Groundhog Day* every day as he, for whatever reason, got mad and tried to get even. He tested every boundary and every rule and became outstandingly angry at being controlled in any way. Discipline is a term which conjures up Draconian images for me, but in reality it neatly sums up the regime I was required to adopt in order for my son to find his way through this huge melting-pot of emotions.

It was a hard and confusing concept for Attila to grasp: that he wasn't master of the universe, or indeed even of his own little world, but grasp it he would, I kept telling myself. For his sake as well as mine. There were, on reflection, a great many tantrums, but tactics were learned and rapidly adopted and we all came through, alive and often quite literally kicking.

But while he needed guidance I needed resilience, a sense of humour, a realistic outlook and the time and ability to be relentlessly repetitive without dying of dementia on the way. No mean feat. What also helped was being honest with a small circle of close friends and giving up any pretence that all was well and I was fine. It released some of the stress, upset and very real pain I felt for both him and myself.

The most useful thing I did learn at this stage was that WIPE gives a good name to a four-letter word. When pushed to extremes and on the verge of letting loose a healthy stream of obscenities, I regularly stood my ground and just repeated WIPE! over and over again. It may have made me look less than normal from time to time but who cares. At least I don't have to listen to my child repeating 'square words' back to me.

In order to reduce the number of daily battles I ended up compiling a list of ten or so completely non-negotiable and unacceptable acts, alongside clear rules and expectations. On these, however tired, I will not budge. On everything else however, dependent on crisis levels, exhaustion levels and circumstances, there is a degree of flexibility and even of possible compromise!

I also became a master of the art of preventative measures and distractions. And if preventative action didn't work I ran through the calamity checklist. Had he had enough sleep? Food? Drink? And if we were having a really bad day I've learned to avoid all unnecessary potentially hazardous situations. Unless the kitchen cupboard is completely bare the supermarket can wait until another day.

From wipe to swipe

Discipline is a little like putting money in the bank: the payoff arrives later, hopefully in this case in the form of good behaviour. But with the arrival of hitting – his, not mine – the thorny question of punishment now entered the arena as I attempted to control his behaviour. All of which leads neatly on to that age-old debate of whether smacking is a good idea or not. The 'it doesn't work' versus the 'sometimes it can'. Personally I struggle in this area. I know that I don't believe in it, but who am I to stand in judgement of others?

Okay, so I'm not perfect and have resorted to it on two occasions. Once, dictated by instinct as my child, when very small, put his hand towards a fire. The other through sheer exhaustion when, having been punched by him once too often, I crossed the fine line and through sheer exasperation I swung, albeit gently, from WIPE to swipe. Neither episode had any effect on his behaviour. It simply shocked and upset me and added tremendously to my sense of guilt. Most of us have been there, whether we choose to admit it or not. And, I suspect, most of us wish we hadn't.

And while we're confessing, yes I have shouted – on a number of occasions. The woman who believes in 'calm and consistent' lost it! Again, something I promised myself I would never do. And yes, afterwards I felt terrible. Did it work? Absolutely not! The result? He shouted back, only louder! But if nothing else I've learned at the end of the day that I remain merely human, not a

Supermum, and perhaps, just perhaps, he learned that I have feelings too.

> 'My son picks on his sister relentlessly and I have to say that I shout a lot. If that doesn't work he is sent to his room, and when that fails I take something away that he really likes. Although whether I manage to stick to that is another matter. Sometimes at the end of the day I'm just so knackered that it's easier to give it back and buy myself half an hour's peace. Although that just results in confusion and I'm left wishing I didn't cave in so easily! When I don't, nine times out of ten, it works.
>
> 'I do also smack my children – as controversial as that is. My son really hurting his sister is what usually drives me to it. The problem is that often a smack is the only thing that can get through to him. Then he cries and apologises – and it does stop him doing it again. Sometimes, afterwards, I feel really, really bad and sit and cry myself. On occasions he has witnessed that too, but I'm not sure it's a bad thing: he gets the message about what his behaviour has caused and then we all have cuddles and get on with life again. I wish he wouldn't do it in the first place, so I didn't have to smack him and feel like that, but he does, it works and he has to learn his actions have an effect.'
>
> *Shyama, thirty-one, mother of Tariq, seven, and Shayla, four*

> 'I've never really managed to get my head around preventative measures and when I was working I found that the weekends were taken up sorting out two-year-old tantrums non-stop. It was as though he was wreaking vengeance for the time I had been away during the

week. We tried the 'naughty chair' but he got used to that too quickly and after a while ran to it, sat down and grinned at me before he'd even finished being naughty!

'I was determined not to smack but sometimes it was all I had left. I've always struggled with it and have used it as a last resort against my better judgement. Normally I put him in his bedroom but it has no lock and these days he just comes straight out again. I end up in a crumpled heap after really monstrous episodes. It's so exhausting. I'm pretty sure that if I was a full-time mother at home, or rather had been in the early days, that I would have been able to develop better strategies for dealing with tantrums and general misbehaviour. Instead I was always trying to hold 101 things together and felt I'd failed us all at the end of the day. In my eyes, mums at home had it all worked out, which I now know is untrue, but at the time that was very much how it felt. Sometimes I simply couldn't take any more and would announce to my husband that I was going shopping for an hour and leave him to pick up the pieces.'

Denise, twenty-nine, mother of Max, six

'Discipline is a nightmare and with three boys under the age of four we've had more than our fair share of it in our house. Public tantrums are also a real treat. These days I try to accept that they are going to happen and deal with them as I would at home, but it does help to pretend that there is no one else around, rather than face the embarrassment of your child behaving like a monster. Rule number one is to ensure that I always win and therefore I never give in. Biting is the worst offence, as far as I'm concerned, although hitting me comes a close second. These days we have a naughty step that the boys have to go and sit on until they are ready to apologise, or I am ready to let them off. When they sit there and fight back I tend to resort to crouching down to their level, holding their arms and, on particularly bad days, shouting at them too. This usually makes them kiss me, hug me and generally grovel for forgiveness, while I just feel like s*** for having shouted in the first place.

'I always swore I would never smack my children but I do when all else fails, which has been known to happen with all of them on a few occasions. It really upsets them but doesn't upset them half as much as it upsets me. I used to feel very bad about it and torture myself for days but now I just think that sometimes it is necessary to get them to stop and listen when all else fails. And ultimately it is never done in a way that could hurt them. It really is far more of a symbol than an actual hurt.'

Marcie, thirty-seven, mother of Thomas, three, Matthew, two, and Nicholas, one

'Our son's worst crime is biting me. He did it a lot just before he learned to talk and then miraculously it stopped. With hindsight I understand it was all part of his frustration at not being able to communicate his needs and desires but I can only tell you that at the time it was horrific. I just sometimes wish that we could raise our children backwards. Then less would be unknown and life would be less of a nightmare!

'Do I ever shout? Oh, yes. The problem is that almost immediately I feel as though I've failed because after all he's just a kid. I only ever smacked him once and then it was more of a pat on the bottom. But six months later he brought the conversation up at supper and said, "Mummy, do you remember the time when . . . ?" F*** was all I could mutter – I hadn't told his father about that one! I denied it and my son looked suspicious, as did his father. What a nightmare when they can talk – it's at moments like that I would willingly return to being bitten!'

Maria, forty, mother of Ben, six

'Lying has to be the thing that I come down on hardest these days. I just won't let any of my children avoid that one if they're guilty of it. The punishment is talking it through and having to listen to me explain how it doesn't serve them, which usually does the trick. I do shout from time to time about other offences and never feel great afterwards. I always regret it, feel as though I'm the only parent in the world that does it and the children always listen more at the end of the day when I just talk.

'I have smacked them from time to time and have to say I don't feel bad about it. It only happens when boundaries have been clearly erected and explained and then overstepped and smacking is a final resort. It's carefully and logically administered and never done in the heat of the moment. That's where the shouting comes in! I asked my six-year-old daughter how she felt about it and she said it was okay because they knew they had been very naughty.

'Thankfully they all seem comfortable with being smacked when necessary – or so I tell myself! Seriously, though, they seem to know that once they have pushed it that far, and are smacked, then that really is the end of the matter.'

Hugh, thirty-seven, father of Sonia, eight, Helena, six, and Theo, three

'Answering back is the worst crime in our house. It just sends me to the edge and back. When my son was a toddler he used to respond to my telling him off by holding his breath and passing out and that was never a pretty sight. When he came round he used to get a clump for the worry he'd put me through! I have smacked them which doesn't worry me at all, but whilst it may not bother me it also has absolutely no effect on them either, so I tend not to bother nowadays. The worst I can do to them is send them to their room and close the door. For some reason they don't open it and come out again, thank God, and it does really have an effect on their behaviour. The day they start opening the door, then I'm in real trouble!'

Barbara, thirty-five, mother of Joshua, eight, and Rebecca, five

Bring in the troops

Monstrous tantrums are hard enough to handle in a two-year-old, but with a five-year-old who's on the big side they're even worse. That, combined with my son's medical history, made outside help seem the only option. Strategies were needed to unlock us from constant combat. The behavioural psychologist taught us many things, not least the vast amount of technical jargon which it is apparently necessary to get your head around before work can begin. Once that was achieved we moved on to 'anger management'. While I may have loathed the terminology, the tricks were effective. We learned to control anger by comparing it to traffic lights! Bizarre but brilliant when your child is obsessed with all things to do with driving. Apparently it is okay to have feelings but getting angry is like driving at a set of traffic lights. You can take it to 'amber' but have to stop there because going through 'red' will only result in a rather painful pile-up. My son really grasped this and having hung the traffic light picture up at home, reminding him to put the brakes on at the beginning of outbursts of rage really did make a significant difference. It didn't work every time but sure as hell helped prevent the odd RTA along the way.

We also did reward charts, although, at the risk of sounding patronising, I would advise being careful in this particular minefield. We were told to set goals such as sleeping through the night without tantrums every two hours, and when this was achieved a star would be stuck on the chart. When he'd won seven stars he'd get a prize –

and not just any old prize but something he really wanted. The problem lay in having to continue this for some time and ran the risk of resulting in a child who was behaving better in many, many ways but expected so much more in others. Leaving a whole new problem to deal with. So approach with caution before generously doling out half the solar system!

The other thing that really helped was his starting at school. He started late, for health reasons, but when he finally arrived it certainly gave him an understanding of the effect of his actions on others and the importance of acceptable behaviour if he wanted to get on. Perhaps that's why he's so angelic at other people's houses and saves the tantrums for home where he knows unconditional love knows no bounds!

> 'The only thing that really worked for us was consistency. When our four-year-old was still climbing into our bed most nights, and kicking us both black and blue in his sleep, we decided we had to act. Until then we'd taken him back to bed when we felt up to it and left him when we didn't, which was most of the time. But the bigger he got the harder it was having him in bed with us. So, after talking to the health visitor, we got firm. We took it in turns, me one night, my husband the next, to take our son back to his bed every time he came in. It only took a week for him to get the message, and the sleep we lost trekking up and down stairs with him was well worth it for the sleep we've made up since then.'
>
> *Carol, thirty-two, mother of Owen, five*

'How to get them to do what you want. It's the oldest problem in the book, isn't it. We tried all sorts of things with our three, with varying degrees of success. Star charts were okay, until we got sick of providing presents every time they got the required number of stars. Threats and bribes were pretty useless too. So were long explanations and serious chats. In the end they took us seriously when they knew we meant business. That is when we stuck to our guns despite pleas, threats, tears and tantrums. But doing that isn't always easy and all too often I'd think is this really worth it? and give in for the sake of peace.'

Gareth, thirty-six, father of Callum, five, and Corin, three

Let's face it, we all get it wrong from time to time, if not significantly more often. Thank God our children are resilient enough to survive our mistakes, blunderings and temporary lapses in control. And thank God they grow up. They tell me that the teenage years can be just as big a challenge to negotiate, but frankly I don't want to know right now. The toddler years have been tough enough and I so want to believe, for as long as I can, anyway, that the worst is over.

Wipe wisdom

- Remember when your child is having a major tantrum and you've tried all else, you could always just give in.
- Unless twenty-four-hour combat holds a certain appeal, don't fight with your kids over the little things. Save

your strength and tactics for the big stuff that really matters, like getting them to bed on time. It's important to ensure you have a couple of sanity-saving hours before you collapse into yours.

- If all else fails try humour. Sticking out your tongue and yelling, 'You're a purple banana,' can work wonders on a truculent two-year-old.

9

Your Money or Your Life

Paid work or domestic slavery – it's your choice

I often feel torn in a society that expects me to be both a career woman and a stay-at-home mum. Whichever way you look at it there's little possibility of simultaneously, and successfully, achieving both. And as much as I may wish I had been born into upper-class society a couple of hundred years ago, the reality is that I wasn't, and juggling work alongside parenthood is an emotional and logistical minefield which I, along with millions of other mothers, have had little choice about negotiating.

It's great that women have the opportunity to work and build a career. But what about the women who'd like to stay at home with their children, particularly when the children are pre-school? That particular opportunity seems to have gone out of the window for many of us. Perhaps my mistake lay in not marrying a millionaire. I have to accept that I got that one wrong and, with small baby in tow, was left with some tough choices to make.

The option, particularly as a lone parent, of staying at home full-time with my son would mean a life of income support, housing benefit, tighter than tight budgets and very few choices. Not a pleasant prospect. I spent a couple of months wrestling with my conscience. Would my son be irreparably damaged by going into childcare? Would we both survive the ordeal intact? Eventually I decided to place him in a local friendly nursery, despite the overwhelming feeling that I was abandoning my baby.

Unfortunately my son developed serious and long-term health problems after only a few weeks. Not due to the care he received, I hasten to add. I was devastated, but in retrospect one good thing did come out of such a horrific situation. I had to give up work and care for him full-time. We may have been broke, but we did get to hang out together and the dilemma of choice had been removed.

Back to work

Eventually he was well enough for part-time nursery and reception class in preparation for infant school and it was time to weigh up the work options once again. Unemployed, self-employed, part-time or full-time? All, I'm afraid, came loaded with pros and cons.

In the end I opted for self-employment, started a business and chose to live with the overhanging shadow of financial insecurity on a daily basis. I must have been, and still am, completely insane. I became a mother, so anything else must be possible I keep telling myself. But I quickly discovered just how hard it is being self-employed. Of course it has its moments, and as I lie here writing in the local park, basking in the first warm day this year before going off to collect my son from school I run the risk of painting a very rosy picture. But the other side? At night I regularly lie awake in the dark and panic about the tax man and a million and one other details, and that on top of a couple of hours' work once he is safely tucked up in bed.

Most of the time, though, it's been the right option for me. There are days, my friends will testify, when I wonder if it will ever get any easier; I often feel like a failure for being tired and broke, overloaded and unmanageable. But no choice is ever going to be perfect and just for today this is the best one available. All I really know is that it is nigh on impossible to manage motherhood alongside a career and simultaneously be successful at both, and that a little guilt along the way is simply part of the parenting package.

'The job I do is relatively difficult for a temp to cover, so following the birth of my son I negotiated with the board and came to a gentleman's agreement. Whilst I would only take two weeks actual maternity leave, after that I could bring my son to work with me for the first eighteen months. I know it's not common and in many ways it's not ideal but it worked brilliantly for us and did mean that we all got pretty close to what we wanted. I was even able to arrive a little late and leave a bit early on days when I was completely exhausted. I was also very lucky in that my nan lived very close and she used to come and help entertain him as he got a little older so I could get all my work done vaguely on time. He then went on to nursery, which coincided with the arrival of number two. That time around I did actually take some maternity leave but with the agreement that I would do some work from home and again my nan helped out.

'When either of the children is ill it has to be said that it's always me who takes time off work to look after them. In fact, anything to do with the kids is down to me. So much so that my husband, despite my encouragement, has still not learned to drive, thereby excusing himself from a lot of the work involved.'

Margie, forty-one, mother of Dane, six, and Mia, three

'I never really stopped working after having my son. Ten days after he was born a friend rang in a panic about a deadline and I remember sitting in front of a computer screen trying to type with my arms stretched out in front of me and my son balanced carefully across them! He wasn't a great sleeper and nothing could be achieved without him attached to me in some way. It was definitely easier at first that I worked from home and could therefore be around a lot more for him, but in some ways that's got harder as he's got older. He's four now and we struggle with the stretchable minute. "Mummy'll be done soon" is the constant phrase, when secretly we both know that Mummy'll never be done.

'When our son is sick and I'm working at home then I carry the bag – quite literally! Although I do think that if I had a major deadline my husband would step in. Having said that we did come pretty close to divorce quite recently and he didn't even know about it. My son and I had both been vomiting from eight p.m. until five a.m. and felt turned inside out. When my husband got up and said, "God, what a terrible night's sleep," I thought that was the end. The bottom line is that when your child is ill and you work then everything stops. You really don't have any option but to look after them.'

Gaynor, thirty-six, mother of Nial, four

'At first I found it okay to leave my baby and return to work. The hardest thing I struggled with was the fact that the others in my office were not as fascinated as I had hoped by my endless conversation about him – funny that! I had programmed myself from the day I got pregnant to know I would return to work so it was relatively easy at that stage, especially as I went back part-time. It got more difficult when he got a little older and was more aware of who was looking after him. He began to get very attached to other people and then I felt it should have been me, and that we were both missing out. In the end I gave up my career and looked after him full-time, which was definitely the right decision for us.

'If he's ill my husband and I share the care. When we were both working it allowed us to do half a day each and at least put in an appearance at the office. But unspoken assumptions do exist. Basically I do the food, the clothes, the school, the practical stuff and my husband decides what I lead him to believe he is deciding for himself.'

Maggie, thirty-seven, mother of Reece, three

'I think my wife thought that a year after each birth she would be ready and happy to go back to work. In reality she found it a great deal harder each time than she had expected. It was made slightly easier, however, by the fact that I worked at home and that took a little of the pressure off, knowing that even if the nanny got it wrong Daddy was there as back-up in some shape or form. When one of them is ill we both take off an equal amount of time to look after them as that seems only fair. Working from home makes that easier too. The only unspoken assumptions in our relationship are that health we deal with jointly, corporal punishment that's my department, she deals with education and the school and I'm very definitely in charge of music matters.'

Lawrence, thirty-nine, father of Leah, seven, Sophie, five, and Charlie, two

'Suddenly this career-obsessed female was thrown headlong into the domestic arena and it wasn't a pretty sight. I can't cook. In fact I hadn't baked a cake since domestic science, aged fourteen. I just didn't do practical. Looking after a baby meant I had to do practical all of the time. Instead of going to work I had to buy nappies, make sloppy food and then try to stop my son from pouring it all over his head. It was like taking very early retirement and being sent away to boarding school all at the same time. Most of my friends had returned to work after having children and I felt left alone. Suddenly I had to fill my day with a whole range of new activities. I attended lots of mother and baby activities – usually only once. I went to a baby gym class and ended up feeling like a dog trainer. I went to a music class but my baby refused to sit still and I felt like I'd been taking part in a low-grade rugby tackle for forty-five minutes. The most successful activity was probably playgroup, but these events are hardly conducive to good conversation. You have to watch your child constantly. Make sure he doesn't fall backwards off the slide, that he doesn't annihilate the church bookstall, that he doesn't snatch, that he doesn't get beaten up in the jungle that is the Wendy house.

'Eventually I stopped putting myself through going to these gatherings, managed to find a few like-minded mums and survived. As time marched on we muddled through together and slowly began to find our retirement more fulfilling. I was lucky enough to have a husband who could financially support us and as a result I was free to learn to appreciate the beauty of every moment more than I had ever done before. There were, I discovered, new spaces in my mind, freed from the stress of work, to enjoy life.

'Yet despite this personal growth there is a huge part of me that has simply had to be put on hold and that has been hard to say the least. The hunter-gatherer in me is now hidden beneath a myriad of other roles, which today come first. I may be a pushy, ambitious, driven individual but I've decided to stay at home with our children. Why? Quite simply because the compulsion to stay with these little things was greater than the compulsion to work. It was a compulsion for me rather than any rational conviction. I don't think there is anything wrong with mothers returning to work so long as the children have good and consistent carers. I just didn't want to miss any of this extraordinary opportunity of experiencing my children so intensely in these early years.

'I have learned so much from being at home and looking after my children. I have learned more about myself, who I am and what I want to be. Free from the intellectual and emotional stresses of work I am able to look out and reflect on the rest of the world. Read a newspaper rather than fill in forms. Brain? Yes, I still have one of those, and whilst I may find my keys, newspaper and coffee in the fridge from time to time, then again I always did.'

Lisa, thirty-four, mother of Hamish, five, Connor, three, and Davy, one

'I had very mixed feelings returning to work following the birth of my first child, but felt that I had to try in order to find out whether it was right for us or not. In reality it has been easier than I had imagined it would be. Having great childcare has made a world of difference and, at the end of the day, I had worked for twenty years and it's part of my make-up to use my brain in order to feel fully satisfied. I try not to feel too guilty about it, although sometimes that's easier said than done, not least when my daughter cries when the nanny goes at night and grins from ear to ear on her early morning arrival, while all I get is the night-time whinges in between. There's a high price to pay but it's the best decision for all of us at the moment.'

Carole, forty-two, mother of Lauren, four

Return of the hunter-gatherer

Having made my decision, during more rational and saner moments I know I don't need to sacrifice everything for my child in order to be a good mother. Today the problem is in a way more practical. I do mothering, then work, then back to mothering, with alarmingly little time to adjust from one to the other. Little sleep tagged on for good measure and the challenge comes in simply switching from role to role. They both operate at such different paces and require such different skills. It's a major achievement if I can put thoughts of my son to one side and focus on the task in hand at work. And it's just as hard sometimes to slow down and pay attention to him when we're together, rather than racing him along at my working pace, with half my mind on the next job to be done when he's in bed.

No doubt there will inevitably come a point when my son's backside is reclining in the psychiatrist's chair and he's moaning about me, and how I got it so wrong. But let's face it, I've done it about my own parents so I suppose it will just be payback time.

I can only conclude that whatever each of us decides to do, the fears, worries, concern and guilt appear to remain part of the parenting package. But perhaps their very presence is what helps keep us on our toes and working towards being good enough parents each day.

There is some strange dividing line. Some parents are home for bed, and some are not. Is this one of the agonising choices of family life, or perhaps a tacit, if unspoken, compromise between those at home and those out at work? There are times when even the most devoted parent feels torn. Having once again rushed home from the office to make it home in time for bed, arriving tired, drained and in need of emotional and physical sustenance on every level, being greeted by a whirlwind of similar wants and needs can be severely taxing. In my own case, coping at the end of the day with the needs of my spouse, six-month-old, eighteen-month-old and three-year-old can be an emotional tinderbox and one must tread carefully if everyone is to make it to bed without tears; and I don't just mean the children.

'"Take my advice," said a colleague, more eighteenth century than twenty-first. "Go to your club after work [I think he meant Boodles or Whites rather than the Ministry of Sound], then arrive home when the children are all tucked up . . . life is so much easier that way." This is a man who calls his current wife Mk3. Not surprisingly Mk1 and Mk2 found life was rather better without him.

'Given the pressures and the chaos of home at bed-time, the idea of a business event at six-thirty p.m. can be tempting . . . Oh dear, Daddy won't be home tonight . . . Oh whoopee, Daddy is going to a conference in Venice this weekend and will we see him next weekend, since Venice is where Mk2s tend to come from in the first place?

'I could stay later in the office, there's always more than enough to do, but I do really want to make it home in time for bed. I want to see my children every day – indeed my family is the very purpose of all my hunter-gathering. I walk through the door wanting so much to meet all their needs, and believe me they're great by that stage, but I feel like an alien who has just walked in from another planet. They are tired. Daddy's suggestions of building Lego are ignored. They want to destruct, not construct. As they begin hurling cushions about the room, nothing useful appears to come out of my mouth: "Um, cushions, I think not . . . gosh, you are having fun . . . did I remember to send that fax . . . must check that share price tomorrow morning . . ."

'"Daddy! Daddy!"

'"Would you like a cup of tea, darling?" asks my wife.

'"Yes, yes, thank you. No, no, I'll make it myself." A few moments to escape. When I return, warfare has been progressing at an alarming pace. Older child is wailing, toddler is looking triumphant (perhaps I was just imagining the horns), the baby has knocked over a glass of milk. "I'll just get a cloth. B*****! I did forget to send that fax."

'The whirlwind that is my family then attempts to move gradually up the house, through the bath and finally into bed. Many a mountain has been climbed, a grizzly bear fought and a potty emptied. Then comes the moment that makes it all worth while. I'm finally tucked up in bed with my children and reading them their bedtime story. As I bend down to kiss them goodnight, I thank God for them. It'll be all right if I send that fax tomorrow, I muse. "Daddy, I need a wee!"

'So I have to take care before I turn the key in the lock, to think for one extra moment, not about my own day, but about those on the other side of the door. They will have had their own ups and downs, and at this moment the return of the hunter-gatherer is perhaps the high point of their day. If I decide, perhaps only through exhaustion and overwork, to be short-tempered and irritable, then home will mirror my mood, but if in my tiredness I open the door full of hope and fun, then the sun shines bright, even at bedtime. But God is it hard!'

With grateful thanks to David Cobb. Reproduced from WIPE *magazine*

'I always found switching from worker to mother very hard. I'd arrive at the childminder's with my head still buzzing with work, and collect a child desperate for my attention. We'd go home, my son chattering non-stop, and for the next couple of hours until bedtime I'd feel exhausted, and horribly guilty that he wasn't getting the best of me. Things improved a lot when I was able to cut an hour off the end of my working day and get home earlier. I also started to go for a ten-minute walk in the park before picking up my son. It gave me the chance to slow down and make the transition which I needed. As soon as we got home I changed out of working clothes into more relaxed ones and had something to eat. All this helped make our evenings much easier and I began to enjoy the play/bath and bedtime routine a lot more.'

Tessa, forty, mother of Jordan, four

The way ahead

In an ideal world, I would have come from Sweden. Smörgåsbord would be a small price to pay for some of the most far-reaching and innovative parental-leave schemes in the world. With relatively long periods of leave, generous income replacement and the flexibility to return to work at reduced hours, what more could a parent ask for? But this is Great Britain and frankly I'm in danger of painting placards and picketing Number 10 as Britain hovers dangerously near to the bottom of the childcare league in the EU.

On the other hand, perhaps we should just charge, although I'm not entirely sure who we'll send the bill to:

Getting out of bed

Weekday rates:
8 a.m. £5
7 a.m. £7.50
6 a.m. £50
5 a.m. £500
4 a.m. £7,500
3 a.m. £10,000
2 a.m. £20,000
(Weekend rates charged at time and a half)

Locating service for socks, book bags, show-and-tell items and special pointy Lego bits

If parent directs child, who finds item: £5
If parent repeatedly directs child who whines 'I can't find

it,' whereupon parent goes and lays hand on item exactly where child was directed to find it: £50
If parent locates same with bare foot: £150
If parent locates same with bare foot before morning slug of coffee: £1,000

Wiping noses
5/£1
Wiping other people's children's noses: £2 each

Nappy changing
£2.50 pee/£5 poo
Convincing partner to change nappy I'll pay £85/hour pee, £450/hour poo, £900 to ball up nappy and throw it away, as well as closing the wipe box lid so they aren't all dried out for next time.

Chauffeuring
Local mini-cab rates apply, with the following provisos:

– Driver must stay in control of radio/tape/cd player at all times otherwise a £10 surcharge will be incurred.
– Driver will referee backseat fights gratis, but pulling over to do same will incur £20 surcharge. Pulling over while grandparent or in-law is in car £500 surcharge. Pulling over while grandparent or in-law is in car on the way to actual birthday or anniversary of same £1,000.

Cleaning
Self: £2.50
Child, entire: £2.50

Face only: £1 (painted, additional £3)
Bottom only: £5
Sick: £1,000
Household: £7/hour
Sorting colourful plastic toy bits into correct containers: £20/thousand

Reading
e.g. *Pat the Bunny* 1–10 times 5p each
11–25 times £1 each
26–100 times £5 each
101+ times £10 each
With funny voices add 5p per voice
For sounding interested add £5
Not skipping words add £10

Always a pleasure, never a chore, no job too small . . .

Whether we go out to work or not, if we're actively taking responsibility for raising our children there's no getting away from the fact that it's damned hard work. Yes, I know it's fulfilling, enriching and life-changing. But it's hard work too. And the answer my son gets to his five hundredth request for a drink/snack/game/video is not always the one I would, in an ideal world, wish to give: 'It'll be a pleasure, darling, no problem.' In reality I regularly snap. 'Not again, absobloodylutely not,' I mutter, before leaving the room and banging my head repeatedly against the kitchen cabinets.

Time out. Frankly I needed it, and still do from time to time. A break from parenting, a little time to recharge my jaded batteries and to remember that I am, despite my doubts, more than just a mother.

I always found it horrendously hard to tear myself away from my son or to put my own needs first. But from time to time I've had to, simply in order to stay sane. After my nerve-racking initial forays into the world of childcare, the eccentric elderly babysitter who put nappies on inside out and the council childminder who came for a limited period only, I've been lucky that my mother has been around, providing utterly safe and reassuring childcare when I needed it. And thank God. I couldn't have done it without her. Actually I could. But it would have been a thousand times more difficult.

My son's father has also provided reliable, loving and safe childcare. We may not have made it past the first two years intact as a couple, but every cloud has a silver lining and this was definitely it. Now my son and his dad get to do their bit of male bonding and I get a night or two off every week to recuperate.

So the only remaining problem is what to do with those precious few hours to myself. Meditate? Go to a yoga class? Visit the theatre or the opera perhaps? Or should I go back to a few of the trendy activities of my youth? The trouble is I wouldn't know where to begin with trendy activities these days. I'm not even sure if the word trendy is an acceptable use of language any longer. Gigs? Festivals? They're all but a distant memory of hot crowds, junk food and the smell of patchouli oil.

Small acoustic venues with candles and proper songs are more up my street today. And a relaxing drink with a girlfriend, followed by a hot bath is as near to nirvana as I'm likely to get.

'I never really took any time out when my daughter was small because it was so expensive and I was saving every penny for childcare costs when I returned to work. As a result I felt slightly mad a lot of the time. I was extremely lucky to have such an easy baby, but it was still hard. In the last five months we've managed one night away without her, when she was left with her old maternity nurse, whom I trust implicitly. Apart from that it's the odd night out for dinner; without those I think my husband would leave me. The difference is that in the past we might have gone on to a bar but these days we give it a wide berth, partly because we're too tired and partly because the babysitter has to get home.'

Rachel, thirty-nine, mother of Tara, three

'I insisted on taking some time out from the children or I would have gone quite mad, and I never felt guilty about doing it. I did check out the babysitters carefully and made sure I trusted them before leaving them with the children. But once I was happy with the arrangements I couldn't wait to go out for a bit of time on my own. I went to exercise classes, sat in cafés reading the papers or went round to friends. I think it kept me human. I need that time on my own, though I went out with my husband too, of course. It was very important to us, and still is, to have an evening out together a couple of times a month.'

Sue, forty-two, mother of Tom, six, and Joe, four

'I found it very easy to think about taking time out, but my wife found it difficult and it often left her feeling very guilty. And when we did actually go out we were left alone, facing each other over the dinner table and that led to the brink of divorce! Having children and then leaving them and getting back to us was hard, but ultimately it took our marriage to a different, closer level.

'Childcare came in the form of a series of nannies, some of whom have been markedly better than others. By far and away the worst were the English ones. The best were the Australian, French and Hungarian.

'Where we went when we did have childcare also radically changed. There were no more gigs, movies, clubs and bars. I found that very hard to come to terms with and I resented it. I struggled with having to plan in advance and was generally appalled that my right to spontaneous decision-making had effectively been taken away.'

Stuart, thirty-nine, father of Dougal, five, and Marcus, three

'Time out? Oh, my God, yes. It was absolutely vital. The places we went to changed and so did the social drinking. I had this horrible feeling that if I drank even a little too much, once I got home and was on duty I'd fall asleep, fall out of bed, knock over a glass of water by the bed which would pour into an electric socket, then the house would burn down and all while I was still asleep. Worse still, I'd live and have to explain it to everyone.

'So many of my decisions today, including when and where to go out, are based on whether or not it will make me a "bad mother". There's nothing worse imaginable to me now. Being a prostitute, a drug addict, Margaret

Thatcher, anything is better than being a bad mother. I'll always be here for my child, even if I have to crawl along the road on my hands and knees to get to him. I suppose, therefore, that I took a little less time out than I might have done!

'And my paranoia wasn't helped by the fact that when I got home my son would sometimes be staring longingly out of the letterbox, or posting little notes or heart-shaped crayon pictures out through it. What could be more guilt-inducing than that!'

Joanna, thirty-four, mother of Seamus, six

One of the biggest disappointments of taking time out was that, when I got home, my son didn't run and throw himself into my open arms before I spun him around and we showered each other with kisses. Nothing Hollywood about my fantasies! In reality he was pleased to see me, but he knows how to pull the guilt card and revels in playing the hard-done-by boy who struts his indignation at being left, however good a time he's had. Probably in the hope that I will cave in and buy my way back into his favour.

We've just about got things sorted between us now. He knows that I have to work, and that he has to put up with it sometimes. And he knows that I'm going to go out occasionally, whether he wants me to or not. And both of those are okay, because what he also knows is that I love him as much as the stars, the moon and the sun all put together (and a little bit more!).

Wipe wisdom

- Whether you go out to work or stay at home, refuse to bury yourself in guilt. Always take regular breaks for important indulgences like getting your toenails painted, or reading the papers in peace.

- Try to avoid comparing yourself to every other parent (tricky, but not impossible). Save energy and concentrate on what's right for you and your family.

- Avoid dispensing guilt treats, like coming home with sweets or, worse still, promising trips to theme parks. Kids latch on to this stuff really fast . . . and before long you'll find yourself having to come through.

- It's a rare breed who gets up in the morning and decides to devote the day to screwing up their kids. So go easy on the guilt and don't forget the bottom line – we're all just doing our best.

10

Chaps in Charge

What really happens when men take over

Short of having a sex change, and even I'm not that committed to my work, the experience of being a dad is destined to remain one of life's little mysteries which I will never be able to describe. The experience of being a mum nervously handing a child over to his father is, however, one I'm very familiar with. The first time I left my son with his dad, when our baby was about three weeks old, only confirmed the fact that I have a split personality. Half of me was worried sick that he'd get it all wrong, the other half was so relieved at the sudden freedom of a trip to the baker's without a small attachment clinging to me, that I could only feel exhilarated. In fact I found myself hoping that he'd have a really hard time, just so that he'd get a taste of what I'd been going through for the past few weeks. 'Hope he does a poo and his dad has to cope with it,' I muttered wickedly to myself, basking in the pleasure of buying a loaf of bread and being able to use both hands to open my bag. And he did, and his dad did – cope, that is. Of course he wanted a gold medal for it, but he coped and that was what mattered.

After we separated he had our son regularly, and still does. And he's turned out to be a fantastic coper and much firmer about boundaries like bedtime and manners than I've ever been. He does manage to leave something behind every time he delivers our son home, but in the end it doesn't really matter. What he's absolutely perfect at is loving our son; he does that with total commitment, and I couldn't ask for more.

And since more dads than ever are doing their share, and regularly taking over, if not running the show, I asked some of them to tell it like it is, from their point of view . . .

'I will never forget the day I was first left in sole charge of my tiny, tiny son. I was almost paralysed with fear but was equally determined not to let on. I gave the game away though when his mother returned and I was caught standing on the doorstep, where I'd been for almost an hour, with baby under one arm and dirty nappy waving in my other hand, proclaiming my ability and talent as a father. It was the first nappy I had done, much less done on my own! If I had to sum up that first couple of hours of being in sole charge – terror followed by extreme pride!

'The first time I had my son for a complete day on my own, I felt terrified by the responsibility and fear that I wouldn't be able to fill up the time and know what to do with him. A couple of hours here and there was okay but a full day was another prospect altogether.

Even now his mother and I have separated I can still panic at a full day, or weekend, stretching ahead of us, but as time has gone on I can stop myself immediately and look back over all the wonderful time we've had together and know that there will never be a minute that we can't fill with something, from the exciting to the mundane.

'I have my son overnight at least twice a week and have also had him living with me full-time, when his mother's been on holiday or was in hospital for a long period of time last year. The trick has always been to let go of the fear and just enjoy every minute of it. The worst bits for me are looking at my watch and realising he has to be taken home soon and that we haven't got that long left together until next time. I even feel like that if the "next time" is tomorrow. The best bit is watching him sleep, and before you laugh cynically it's not just because then I can rest but also because he looks so peaceful and beautiful. Even after six and a half years I still go into his bedroom every night he's with me and just look at him for a few minutes. That's such a great feeling.

'I'm in no doubt that my son treats me differently to his mother. And if I had a choice I'd opt for the father figure role every time. Thank God I'm the dad. Traditionally we're definitely seen as more fun and that has to be a good thing, which lets me off the hook a bit. At the end of the day, even though we see each other an enormous amount, it's still like play for him to be left with his dad. If I've learned anything about being a dad it's to make everything as enjoyable for your children as possible. It makes parenting a lot less hard work. And bribery works well too!'

Richard, forty-three, father of Peter, six

'The birth was a strange experience. I wanted to be there, and I wanted to run like hell too. I found a compromise in the end, by nipping out at regular intervals to stock up on food supplies and gulp a few deep breaths. When my son arrived I was overwhelmed with love, and I have been ever since. The first time I had him on my own it was only for a couple of hours and a bottle of milk was enough to keep him happy. But it's got more challenging since then! I work flexible hours and my wife works too, so I do plenty of the day-to-day childcare. My favourite part is putting him to bed. He's four now and curling up with him on his bed for a story and then kissing him goodnight as his thumb plugs into his mouth is still blissful.

'I wouldn't say childcare is easy. I've had to learn so much and I still feel like a novice. But it's very, very worth while. A few months ago my wife went to see friends for a weekend and my son and I had four days together. At times it was tough, but mostly it was funny and touching. I came downstairs one morning to find he'd snipped open every individually wrapped dishwasher tablet in the box and opened all eight yogurts from the fridge, eating a couple of spoons of each. Then he'd cut the mane off his toy lion and snipped off his felt dinosaur's spikes. Of course I ticked him off and he stared at me solemnly while I did, and then said, "But we still love each other, don't we, Dad?" What could I do, except hug him and say, "Course we do."'

Jim, forty-seven, father of Matteo, four

'I just didn't feel ready to be a dad when my girlfriend got pregnant. I felt too young, too ignorant and too scared. But there was no going back, and I wasn't going to walk away from the responsibility. I knew that if I had a child in the world I had to be there. It was a struggle at times, but she's five now and I'm still here, feeling about fifty years older and wondering how a person so small can turn your life upside down.

'We have a lot of fun together. I take her to the park on Saturdays so that her mum can have a break and we talk about life and the world, sitting on a park bench in between sessions on the swings. She's so wise. And she unnerves me by talking about "when I lived before". I think she's a reincarnated princess, judging by the standard of service she expects from us.

'I find it quite hard to get angry with her, but a few times I've really lost my temper and shouted and then she looks at me, eyes full of tears and lip wobbling and I feel like a monster. So it never lasts long.

'I don't know how I'm going to deal with her having boyfriends, I just have to think about it to feel all my protective hackles rise. How will anyone ever be good enough for my girl? And how can any man ever live up to her dad?'

Joe, twenty-seven, father of Betsy, five

'We nearly lost our daughter during a very problematical birth and from the first moment I saw her I was so grateful she was alive, and loved her so much, that I've never felt any fear about looking after her and being able to care for her properly. At the risk of sounding arrogant I've always felt competent to do it. The big joke in our house was always about how good I was at changing nappies, at least when Cherry was still being breast-fed. The day she transferred to solids and the nappy contents changed in both consistency and aroma – beyond all recognition – was the day I resigned. I never changed a nappy from that day forth! Give me bottles to sterilise, clothes to wash, sick to clean up and it will all get done, although the dog would sometimes beat me to it on the latter. But a baby on solids and a nappy to change and suddenly I was back at the office.

'My first full day, and in fact overnight, of being in sole charge didn't scare me. More surprisingly, it didn't seem to worry my wife either. We'd always been quite a good double act so I don't think she had too many fears about me being able to manage on my own.

'My wife and I separated when Cherry was six and as a result I've had to have my daughter on my own a lot more than I might have done. At first I was very conscious of Cherry having to get used to two homes. My wife and I took great care to explain to her that the changes were about Mummy and Daddy and not about her, and that she would always be very loved in both of our homes, but I still overcompensated a great deal at the start. Most of our time alone together was spent buying toys and clothes for her and generally overindulging her to a ridiculous degree. I put myself out an enormous amount for her too, always ensuring our days were action-packed and involving her friends in as many of these "fun" activities as I could. There were times back then when I did struggle, when I did think I had to fill every waking moment with wonderful things to do. These days we're more than happy just to sit and spend time together. What I've learned is that she's usually happy to be with me, just hanging out at home together.

'If I'm truly honest I have to confess to feeling quite relieved when I hand her back to her mother after a weekend. I suppose that's because I no longer have the constant responsibility, although it is easier now as she gets older and needs less input in certain ways.

'The best bit about being a chap in charge is just being with her and laughing a lot. There's nothing better than being with her as she climbs up the steep learning curve.

'The worst aspect of being on my own with her is sometimes, particularly when I'm busy at work, I would literally just like to go to bed in the evening, but now she's thirteen I have to stay up late because she's not about to be packed off to bed. Also there are times when I get invites to somewhere I'd really like to go, or to do something I'd really like to do and I can't go. But I've never regretted having her or resented it for a moment. My life fits in with seeing Cherry and not the other way around.'

Andy, forty, father of Cherry, thirteen

'When first left in charge of my first child . . . It was completely exhilarating and terrifically exciting. I remember being really delighted about being able to muck around with my baby for the first time on my own. There had always been some kind of sense before that she'd been the property of her mum, or the nanny, but this time she was mine. I introduced her to *Exile on Main Street* which seemed like an appropriate thing to do, and it worked. She's definitely a Stones fan now. Even whole days and nights on my own with her weren't overwhelming. Well, perhaps just a little. But the prospect of them was okay.

'I remember being a bit freaked out at not being able to stop and take time out if I felt like it, and later that first evening I suddenly realised what it was to be completely powerless over another person. Nothing I could do had the effect that I wanted, which in this case was for her to stop crying. It was the middle of the night and it had gone on for hours. I remember the mystification turning to anxiety, turning eventually into anger, and as I held her I imagined how easy it must be for single parents living in foul conditions on virtually nothing to lose their rag and throw them against the wall. It seemed like an eminently sensible option at the time. Needless to say I resisted temptation, put her down and went back to bed.

'From that moment on I was a devotee of the school of hard knocks. She was okay and could therefore be left on her own. Once I'd reached the conclusion that this was just a little human being exercising and that was all there was to it, then I just let her get on with it. I think mothers do perhaps doubt our competence to a degree. Although having said that, my wife fully expected me to be able to cope and take on my fair share of responsibility and as a result she had no qualms about leaving me in charge. In fact she regularly told me I was a great dad. Although perhaps that was a ploy to encourage my new-found enthusiasm at being in control!

'If the truth be known there have been occasions, here

and there, when I've been well and truly bollocked when she's come back and I've apparently "done something wrong". Personally I think I'm just your typical man and, as a result, less finickity about things such as "sell-by" dates. Tidying up after us was never a strong point either. In fact it wasn't long after our first one was born that I realised I had to moderate my behaviour if we were to live in anything approaching harmony.

'And then there were two. Having one child to be in charge of was one thing, having two you can go for "man-to-man marking" but then there were three and that definitely required a shift to a "zonal defence strategy". The best bit about being a dad and being in charge is hanging out with a mate who always agrees with you. With the exception, of course, of when a degree of discipline is required. Dads definitely get more hero-worshipped than mums, and that's fine by me.

'The hardest bit of being on my own with one, two or all three of them? Probably the hardest thing is just to change gear and slow down enough to be at their pace and not expect them to keep up with me operating at my usual rate. The worst thing? I don't know. I can't think of anything.'

George, thirty-six, father of Natasha, five, Jonty, four, Gabriel, two

'The biggest fright I had was the time I took my five-year-old off to the shops to buy some sweets. His mum had gone off for a weekend at a health spa and left the two of us together for a bit of male bonding. So I figured the sweet shop was a good place to start. I was, unfortunately, on crutches, as I'd recently broken my leg falling down a couple of stairs. So when I realised, halfway to the shops, that I'd forgotten my reading glasses, I wasn't about to nip back for them. Anyway, my son chose a bag of sweets and off we went, me hobbling, small boy munching at my side. But after six or seven of these sweets he announced that they weren't very tasty.

'When we arrived home I retrieved my reading glasses and had a look at the packet. To my horror I discovered that the bag was in fact a large packet of bangers. Those small explosives we used to set off as kids by hurling them at high velocity on to the pavement! Panic ensued. My wife returned later to discover an empty house and a note saying "gone to hospital". My son and I later returned from a lengthy stay in casualty with the wise, if rather obvious, recommendation from the doctor that he shouldn't jump up and down for a while. Perhaps chaps in charge should only be so when wearing their reading glasses.'

Michael, forty-eight, father of Thomas, five

Confessions of a househusband

All very well when the chaps take over for the odd hour or two or even a day or two. But what happens in families where Mum and Dad decide to reverse roles? What does Dad get up to with the offspring while Mum is out at work? I asked househusband Paul Godwin Brown to fill in some of the details . . .

'Before we start I'd like to take this opportunity to say that Fiona is a lovely woman, and I can't be half bad as she's been married to me for seven years, or nine years, or something like that!

'It was a shock to wake up one day to find that I had become a househusband. Yes, we had discussed it at length; my CV was somewhat patchy, lacking those blue chip things that employers look for, while my wife's was an impressive deep blue hue of the advertising world's finest. It all made perfect sense. Even so, it was difficult coming to terms with the fact that I was having the time of my life.

'Here I am at the door saying goodbye to my well-dressed, highly proficient wife, watching as she marches purposefully to the Tube bound for the West End, waiting until I can assume the earnest role of dad. What a sham we males have to go through, pretending we've grown up into responsible adults. What a relief to be able to revert!

'First things first. What toys to yank out of those wicker baskets? Well, it's got to be the train set, hasn't it? My son Thomas starts at one end whilst I start building at the other. An argument over the placing of the level crossing is quickly resolved and soon we have trains chugging around the room. To assist with atmosphere, various suitable CDs have to be played. We've found Pink Floyd invariably does the trick. Tracks like "Welcome to the Machine" from *Wish You Were Here* and "On the Run" from *Dark Side of the Moon* are sublime. Much better than those wishy-washy *Thomas the Tank Engine* tapes. Naturally you need to be able to crank up a good sound system to get the full percussive Clapham Junction effect. A small multi-coloured children's tape recorder will not do.

'Fed up playing trains (there are only so many times Noddy can survive being tied to the tracks) we decide to play a more active game called HEAD. This involves Thomas being swung vigorously by his legs around whatever room we happen to be in at the time. "You couldn't swing a cat" is applicable to a number of our rooms. I don't recall the estate agents mentioning this when we were shown around. However, we have learned not to play this game in the bathroom or top bedroom. When Thomas starts shouting, "Head, Head," in front of Fiona, she interprets this as "I have a pain in my". I've yet to give her a comprehensive demonstration of this most requested of activities.

'HEAD is a game I would heartily recommend to other dads with small offspring. It requires good hand to eye coordination, cardiovascular fitness and due to the constant request for more, leads to excellent upper body development. Obviously, rather like swimming, it shouldn't be undertaken immediately after a meal, and you should start with a gentle width rather than the ultimate 360 degree swing complete with release and catch. It's a unique game that really separates the dads from the mums.

'Games over, it's time to turn our attention to grooming, in preparation for a visit to the shops. How is it that everybody else's children look well scrubbed and immaculately turned out whereas Thomas is permanently having a big hair day, and I mean big, especially at the back where it gives a nod to the sixties beehive? Fashionable then, but strange when located on the back of a two-and-a-half-year-old's head. No matter how slickly

I hive it down it just reappears in minutes. I refuse to accept I have hit the househusbanding glass ceiling and hit back with some hair sculpting mud (from a spiky phase my wife went through some years ago). Effective, certainly, but ridiculous when applied to the hive in isolation so I opt for the fully sculpted look.

'I get Thomas into his buggy and we set off for the shops. We do this at a jog partly because Thomas is a confirmed speed merchant, and partly because he now resembles something that isn't altogether human. Presumably because he can no longer feel the wind in his hair the chant of "faster, faster, faster" starts up. Picking up speed, we charge around the leafy streets, perfecting the art of two-wheeled-centrifugal lean as we accelerate into the small few bends, mindful of the need to maintain as much speed and momentum through them as possible. Using this technique we offset the serious disadvantage of our old four-wheeled chassis technology; supposedly faster three-wheeled designs are cut up and left trailing in our wake, all of them in the end pathetically underpowered.

'Triumphant and hyperventilating only slightly, we head for the nearest toy shop. After an earnest discussion on the merits or otherwise of a wooden digger, we leave brandishing a three-foot-long plastic rocket launcher. I realise that the purchase might not have been brilliantly conceived as the "something that isn't altogether human" fires a rocket at the first buggy we come across.

'Back home, and Thomas settles down to prepare some dastardly fate for Noddy involving the new rocket, some tweezers, and lots of ceramic baking beans.

'Bruised, but unbowed, it's time to go scavenging together for leftovers in the fridge. This is a core skill that needs to be developed at an early age, and is so often overlooked by less ambitious carers. Two bacon sandwiches slathered down with brown sauce and an ice cream later, I pause to consider whether that constitutes a balanced diet. An unwelcome pang of guilt washes over me so we both chew lamely on an apple. The half-eaten apple is placed at the top of the kitchen bin while the incriminating evidence of our ice cream feast is carefully buried to avoid possible detection and unwanted interrogation.

'Thomas now heads for his cot, leaving me with a couple of hours to myself. Being a househusband does immediately put one into an exclusive and vaguely exotic league. Invitations to join all-female book clubs, for example, have to be sifted and considered carefully. I wonder whether I should start the redecoration of the top bedroom and bathroom, but decide instead to crack on with the latest offering from the book club.

'The baby monitor and a rather ominous thump alerts me to the fact that Thomas, fed up with waiting for his dad to get him up, has decided to throw himself out of his high-sided cot. It always strikes me as impressive what a large slug of adrenaline can do for the under-exercised, over-thirty-five-year-old. Taking the stairs at an overly ambitious four steps at a time, I miss my footing on the third bound and plant my head on the recently stripped, waxed and varnished planks. Feeling slightly confused I stagger onwards only to be met by Thomas calmly walking past me on his way downstairs.

'Demonstrating an embarrassingly familiar knowledge with the machine, Thomas proceeds to put on his favourite Noddy video, probably to check that the irritating little man and his bell survived his earlier encounters with the train track. Reassured that our hero has survived unscathed, he settles down for a half-hour of viewing. I resist the temptation to lose myself in some car magazines (how to get out of purchasing an estate car is my current project) and go to prepare supper for when Fiona arrives home.

'I've been on a steep learning curve when it comes to food preparation. However, things are improving. My wife continually reminds me that meals always taste much better if you don't cook them yourself, which is just as well because after two years' practice some of my offerings, despite Delia and Nigella's best advice, are still a masticatory challenge. Fine if you have a strong set of ivories, but expensive when the household is blighted with cusps and crowns that capitulate and ping off at the slightest sign of a fight.

'Time ticks on and with supper and bath time approaching I start to prepare the house for Fiona's homecoming. Toys are stuffed under chairs; books are left out to illustrate the intellectual rigour of our day. Mentally I begin to make the metamorphosis from Irresponsible Big Kid Playing Hooky to Responsible Husband and Model Father, a process assisted by a large glass of Sauvignon Blanc. I settle back and wonder when Thomas will become old enough for a remote-controlled plane. I did so want one when I was little.

'Do I think it is as exhausting as women make out? I

think for many women it is exhausting, but not for me. I probably do half the work they do. I've managed by being fairly lazy. In fact the most difficult things over the last few years include sometimes being ignored at dinner parties when I say what I do, or if other guests do want to talk, finding to my horror that I really don't have too much to say that is interesting.

'Without a doubt the last four years have been the happiest of my life. It's the best job in the world. It's simply unfortunate that it's unpaid, or rather that the school we have chosen insists on charging.'

With grateful thanks to Paul Godwin Brown. Reproduced from WIPE *magazine*

11

A Moveable Beast

Travelling? Don't forget the kitchen sink

Prepare for expansion in every area of your life from here on in. That's about the size of it. Fatter feet (why does that happen?), fatter arse, fatter handbag, fatter car, fatter just about everything. And when children arrive life not only swells but also changes pace quite dramatically too. Gone are the days of fast cars and fast women, or even being a fast woman, and welcome to life in the bus lane. Frankly, the rollercoaster of parenthood is my fastest form of transport these days.

'I'll just carry on as normal,' I told myself pre-childbirth. 'Of course it's possible to go out without the entire house and all its contents coming with us, topped off by a nervous breakdown.' How wrong I was. Until now that is. My son will for ever resent the publishers for commissioning this book. Why? Because today it has caused me to assess the contents of my handbag before casting an eye over the rest of our material trappings. Right here, right now, I'm undergoing my own mini revolution. The battle lines are drawn. His stuff – his side of the door! Civilisation absolutely everywhere else.

From here on in when the plastic horrors enter the sitting room they leave the second they lose their entertainment value. We're going minimalist. I've even gone as far as booking the council's refuse collectors. Tomorrow the oldest sofa, along with its equally elderly throw will be gone. Throws make me feel like a student and frankly I'm sure my son must have reached an age by now where he's past the risk of hurling his Ribena over every piece of furniture, every time.

This decision, or rather the chaotic clutter that inspired it, has been building for a while now. It began on approximately the day my son was born. And now, six years on, it appears to have escalated out of control. The problem was that I was too busy to see it, much less control it. The house began to burst at the seams, while the rules of travelling turned inside out as we developed an unstoppable urge to lug superfluous crap along in our wake.

My handbag and the annihilation of its orderly content was the first to go, and the problem grew from there. The addition of a nappy bag was the first nightmare. Frankly, before I even get to the contents I'm fascinated by quite why they need to be as ugly as sin. I may not be a fashion queen but taste doesn't automatically die with the birth of a child. Floral and tartan prints in a selection of odious and repellent shades just don't do it for me, or indeed match anything I own. So I'm afraid despite losing the niftily attached changing mat, the nylon nightmare was discarded within days and my own handbag merely transformed into a substantially larger version of its former self.

But just how much stuff is it possible to take with us? And did any one of the antenatal classes advise us to take up weightlifting to build upper body strength before birth?

Handbag hell

Pre-baby *(Sure signs of a free and independent woman)*	**Post-Baby**
Diary	Diary, Pen
Pen	Complete make-up kit, Perfume
Lipstick	Keys, Wallet, More Cigarettes
Perfume	Nurofen
Keys	Small plastic dinosaur
Wallet	Glasses (I've aged)
Cigarettes	Mobile (just in case)
Condoms (still unopened!)	Bag of parking meter change
	Nappies x 3, Wipes
	Vest, Spare outfit for the baby
	Change of clothes for the toddler
	Milk for the baby, Juice for the toddler
	Calpol, Selection of antibiotics
	Tissues (used)
	Pot of baby food, Packet of rusks
	Raisins for toddler
	Sliced apple for toddler
	Camera (just in case)
	2 x Thunderbird rockets
	3 x Matchbox cars
	Unidentified piece of 'matter'
	Hat for baby, Hat for toddler
	Gloves for all three of you
	And for an overnight stay:
	Travel cot
	Entire contents of wardrobe
	Football, Kite, Wellingtons
	Sterilising kit, Tins of formula
	Bottles, Whole packets of nappies
	Yet more wipes
	and a cuddly toy . . .

Do we just take too much stuff or were we simply badly designed? Either way, don't try this alone – get staff! You'll never manage with only the normal human quota of two hands.

'My handbag contents? You've got to be joking. How long have you got? Before children I spent more money on my handbags than I would a whole outfit. Today they're wrecked. One box of jelly sweets. Tissues, some used. Car keys – the most important things in my life after the children. Wallet. Purse. Lottery tickets – I live in hope. A camera – in case I see Robbie Williams! A diary with Ant and Dec's autographs! One lipstick box but no lipstick. Handcream. A school notice requiring me to put another fiver in an envelope. Money-off coupons for items I don't want – but hand in and chance my luck. A tin of Vaseline – don't ask! One glove. One cotton bud. Felt-tip pens. Sunglasses case – no glasses. And in the zip-up compartment – the most important – Tampax and a photo of my kids!'

Ruth, thirty-five, mother of Lily, nine, and Ben, six

'Credit cards, money, coins, bubble gum or cigarettes dependent on addiction levels, perfume to hide cigarette smell, Infacol, wipes, some dirty, half-eaten milky bar, felt tips and a plastic man.'

Sally, thirty-three, mother of Jake, four

'Do you have a while? Now I'm a mother I have a series of large handbags and also of appointments with the osteopath. Seriously, I put my back out by humping around vast quantities of crap I thought we might possibly need with every move we made, and now even drag the huge bags to the osteopath to repair the damage on a weekly basis! She says I should get rid of them, so now I put a small bag inside the big bag and leave the big one outside when I see her! The auxiliary handbag is a little like a caravan being pulled by a mum. It has an entire change of clothes in it for my son, and one for me in case vomiting occurs, KitKats, chews, a set of twelve markers, several books, racing cars (not quite full-size thankfully), the usual receipts, lottery tickets (please God let me get lucky this week and have staff by next), and what is supposed to be parking meter change in the bottom, but in reality is what I've raided from his allowance for just such a purpose.'

Jane, thirty-six, mother of Tom, three

'Absolutely organised. Nothing strange in it. That's why I have a nanny.'

Rebecca, thirty-three, mother of Caroline, four, and Nicholas, two

Buggy off

Then there is the addition of the buggy to our lives. Off-road Robin Reliant or whopping great Victorian perambulator? Both have their plus points, not least the latter's ability to mow down anyone in your path, but at the end of another long day it's yet another accoutrement to be folded and unfolded, dragged and lugged around for the next year or two. I spent a great deal of time in the early days loading everything I could possibly think of into and on to it, based purely on the worry that I would have forgotten the one thing I needed and therefore had to take everything we owned everywhere with us every time.

My biggest buggy headache was ambitiously walking to the shops, then, as the C-section scar became just too uncomfortable, attempting to take the bus home. Ah. Only two hands. With small baby, three bags of shopping, a handbag, nappy bag and buggy in tow I didn't stand a hope in hell of simply collapsing the buggy, much less of getting the entire collection on to the bus before it began to move off. And even if I did achieve the impossible, why, why, oh why weren't the buggy or the bus's luggage deposit built to fit together in any way, shape or form? The designers of public transport clearly don't do joined-up thinking or perhaps I just got the wrong buggy or the wrong bus. Whatever the reason, it never ceased to leave me standing amazed and still lugging small baby, buggy, bags . . .

I'm only grateful for one thing as far as buggies are concerned. Namely, that I had only one child. Having attempted to transport my own plus a friend's two, I can imagine little more taxing, both physically and logistically, than pushing two children in a double buggy with a third swinging precariously on the attached skateboard step, while carrying bags and all the necessary paraphernalia of parenthood. And as for the required upper body strength – I am afraid I simply don't make the grade. If I ever do have a temporary lapse of sanity and have more children I shall certainly train as a shot putter first.

'My only complete conviction about buggies is that you should never attempt any form of public transport with them. It may be called "public" but it's impossible to use with small kids and a buggy. So much so, in fact, that since having my children my bum has been glued to the seat of my car in order to ferry everything around with the minimum of inconvenience. My kids now think it's a real treat to go on the bus. The thing I hate most about buggies has to be how filthy they get and how there's nothing you can do about it. I did, however, find one that was fantastic because I could hang stuff on the back and it was so sturdy it didn't tip. There had to be a downside though and the price I was prepared to pay was yet again a high one. Try as I might, it wouldn't fit into my boot. I sacrificed a sports car for an Astra just for the sake of a buggy – that's how bad it gets.'

Fiona, thirty-nine, mother of Jamie, seven, and Maddie, five

'The hardest thing for me was that I was completely besotted with my child and ended up furious that I couldn't look adoringly at him when he was in the buggy. Everyone else could see him and there I was left pushing behind, like some sort of servant. I mostly hated them, though, because they are designed entirely for the baby and take absolutely none of your needs into consideration, I mean, where is the fitted cup holder for your coffee? Also they're too short. And, having provided all-weather cover and cosiness for your child, there's nothing to stop you, meanwhile, being completely soaked and cold. For me that conjures up an image of exactly what happens to you when you become a parent.'

Pam, thirty-nine, mother of Jake, seven

'If you have siblings who are near contemporaries, you may find mobility a hurdle. There are twin-seater pushchairs or double buggies but strangely these aren't motorised like golf buggies or even lawnmowers.

'Women sporting upper arms like Dolph Lundgren and the buttocks of a shire horse are more often than not the pushers – or ex-pushers – of double buggies. They can also permanently affect the way women walk. The forward lean to take the strain results in many women years later still walking at an apparently unfeasible forward angle with their faces only inches from the pavement.

'Fortunately, Daisy was just out of her buggy when Jack was ready for his inaugural trip. So no double buggy required. Daisy rides behind on a "buggy board" – a bit like the footplate man on an old steam loco, or Boadicea in her war chariot.'

With grateful thanks to Mark Whitaker. Reproduced from WIPE *magazine*

'If I'd only had one child I would have rather carried them. What is it with buggies that makes them so impossible to clean and therefore always so filthy, and why do the wheels always go? I had my daughter in a pram when one of the wheels flew off. On top of that they're always too low for me. Adjustable handles, that's what we need.'

Claire, forty, mother of Elsie, seven, Eleanor, five, and Harry, two

'The only good thing about buggies is Pram Pusher's Arms, more generally known as the suntan I get from fingertip to elbow as I push relentlessly, my arms stretched out in front of me. The downside – oh, there are many. They tip over, hats fall over your child's face and you can't see them to know, they're filthy almost instantly and the most fun of all – the karate chop. When your child won't get into the buggy and they go completely rigid the only option is to karate chop them and whilst they buckle, momentarily in shock, to slot them in and strap them up at high speed. There's just a split second to complete the whole manoeuvre – highly skilled stuff, parenting!'

Penny, forty-two, mother of Della, eight, and Eddie, six

Simple pleasures

The supermarket. Not high on the list of pleasurable activities for many of us I should imagine. So just how far down have I gone, to what depths have I plunged, when I crave an outing to the supermarket ALONE? On my own is a luxury nowadays and I long for nothing more than the simple pleasure of buying our food without first having to assess whether my son's mood will make the experience tolerable (unlikely), ghastly (a lot more likely) or torturous (almost definitely).

If I had more than one child I'd clearly have to chain the tribe to the trolley. Thankfully these days I simply plant my son firmly in the trolley itself and slowly bury him under the supplies. That way I know where he is, no more items are randomly grabbed from the shelves (by him that is; I still randomly grab – it's quicker that way) and he gets to pretend he's Michael Schumacher all at the same time – a hat trick.

I want my MGB

These days for such complex manoeuvres as the supermarket and the school run, and indeed the taxi service I appear also now to operate, the bus just doesn't cut the mustard. But a regular car for all that paraphernalia? Surely it has to be possible, or do we really all have to aspire to, or worse still resort to an MPV? I'm sorry but the best that can be said about them is that they're deeply unattractive. I accept it's a personal view but I don't believe there's one of you out there, not even a politician with all the spin, who could persuade me otherwise.

I understand that when you have a tribe they are probably practical but if that's the case then I remain grateful again that I have only the one. I could have had a career as a school bus driver, been around children and even got paid for it, should the desire to drive such a vehicle have been overwhelming. Why would I want an MPV? I want my MGB. That'll be the MGB we don't have at the moment! But the point is that we could have a two-seater and for that I am grateful. My father, as an ex-racing driver, was passionate about cars and often used to tell me that if you could fit the child in the footwell then there was space enough. Or on the back parcel shelf – now that was luxury! And even today the smell of old car leather seats brings the memories of what a family car should be flooding back. I stand firm in the knowledge that he was right.

What amazes me is how, regardless of the size of the car, we manage to find enough rubbish to fill it, and, what's more, convince ourselves that it's all necessary. Whether the trip is short or long it's inevitably packed to the gills. I'm working on that from here on in. Do I really need a boot full of sports kit, a long-redundant travel cot, footballs, kites, clothes for every weather condition known to man . . . It sounds like the conveyor belt on the *Generation Game* after a while. If I'm honest I think I've been making it a whole lot more complicated than it ever needed to be. First-time motherhood fuelled me with panic but the fact is that we would have got by without whatever items I considered essential whenever I left the house. And I only have to open the boot these days to face hard facts. It has become quite simply another storage cupboard from the house overflow.

Born to be wild

Sixty-eight thousand pounds, give or take a few pence. That's all I ask for. With an expanding family I don't require an expanding car, rather an accommodating bank manager. I wasn't a hatchback girl before I had a child and I'm not about to become one now. What I'm after is the iris-blue Porsche 911 Carrera Cabriolet charitably donated by Porsche GB for a week to establish its potential as a family car. Not an obvious choice, I agree, but frankly I could convert anything this captivating to almost any purpose.

This particular 911 joined the Porsche model range in spring 1998. My only question is why did it take me this long to manoeuvre a road test? In technical terms it's one of the safest convertible sports cars on the market at the moment, but I'll just stay focused on the girl things. Cruise control and heated seats appeal a lot! Although I'm the first to admit after this week that the latter is possibly not the most practical extra for a family car. Chocolate ground into the 'ruffled leather' would be bad enough, but melted? Now that's an altogether more challenging problem.

Four-letter expletives were repeatedly muttered upon the arrival of the Carrera into our modest family life. All from my lips, I confess. My son just froze with sheer delight, but by the time its wheels touched the ground, fresh off the delivery lorry, rest assured it took no time at all for me to recover composure, and with the mere flash of an indicator I was the most marketable mum in town. The school run, the supermarket, McDonald's drive-thru, in fact all previously humdrum activities suddenly became completely necessary at increasingly regular intervals as parental life shifted up a gear to the high life.

The first school run was reminiscent of the *Krypton Factor.* Two parents, two children, two buggies and a number of assorted essential accessories and one small space was nothing less than testing. After much pushing and prodding, removing and restacking, the answer lay in roof off and two small children in the back with rain covers and buggies pinning them safely down. It restricted their view somewhat, but kept them safe. Delighted shrieks filled the air. On arrival home, however, the four wind-bludgeoned humans unfolded themselves and entered the house to survey the damage. I consoled myself in the knowledge that children generally shriek when you brush their hair at the best of times, and as for the adults, what's a little pain among parents? It has proved to be a family car. Fling the buggy in the back – just remember to leave the children at home.

Next the supermarket challenge. Comfortable and extremely stylish run, no doubt about it, and it didn't take as long as usual; the number of male drivers willing to let a woman in a convertible pull out made all the difference. In no time at all it was mission accomplished. Roof off and seventeen bags of loosely packed goodies fit perfectly under the bonnet. It is worth remembering, however, that two to three items per bag is the limit, and I would advise only buying soft things as they seem to compress more easily.

A visit to the drive-thru McDonald's was an essential part of testing the 911's adaptability to family life, and it was here that I nearly came unstuck. Suddenly the fear of tomato ketchup and apple pie on the seats overwhelmed me. I could fast become a highly neurotic, control-freak-type mother if this were my family car. But no hurdle is insurmountable when sporting seventy grand's worth of incentive. So a 911 Carrera is, in my humble motherly opinion, a perfectly feasible family car. Extravagance with an element of mental challenge thrown in for good measure. This evening I shall be designing a prototype for a buggy that folds in four and stands a chance of fitting under the bonnet.

One word of caution, however. I would advise against extended family outings. Two grandparents wedged securely in the back had to be tried but we probably wouldn't be able to persuade them to repeat the experience. After surgical removal of the bodies, Granny's hairdo was clearly in need of some touching up sooner rather than later and Grandpa's footprints remain for ever imprinted in the deep pile of the rear carpet.

My most memorable moment of the week came during a carefully arranged child-free spin as a handsome young man pulled up next to me at the lights, wound down his window and announced that I looked the part. Well, what a relief. Until then it hadn't crossed my mind that I might look as if I'd stolen it. A Porsche is clearly my destiny. I knew it all along. I pulled away, leaned back and flicked on the cruise control and dreamed of permanent Porsche parenting.

Trains, planes, automobiles and sick bags

So we master the art of the food run, school run, taxi run . . . But what of longer journeys and the prospect of 'Are we nearly there yet?' ringing out over 'The Wheels on the Bus Go Round and Round' for the fortieth time. Or public transport? Even better. Is there anything worse than a train journey these days as a method of transport? Yes, a train journey with a carriage full of families. Frankly a bid to ban the promotion of family railcards would be a smart and sensible move. The adverts show happy, smiling families brimming with self-control. But remember, these are the folk who drive away from the shoot in their self-contained MPV. In short, families should not be encouraged to travel on trains. They fill a whole car so they're not wasting petrol and they'd reach their destination in half the time. Besides which, they wouldn't irritate the hell out of other people on the way there.

At this point I would like to point out that I do in fact include myself in this. As a parent I have become almost immune to my own child's noise but it has made for an easier passage through life to bear in mind that the noise of other people's children still grates. My son, on the rare occasions I have had the nerve or necessity to travel on the train with him, tends to keep himself amused by playing guards and tries valiantly to collect other passengers' tickets. Humorous to a point but the joke soon wears thin and is completely annihilated after three hours or so.

On reflection our last train journey to Disney was not so bad. However, I live in the, albeit vain, hope that the owners of Eurostar will one day change the rules and ban businessmen from trains going via Disney. I think all that needs to be said is that children going to Disney are inevitably going to be excited.

'I thought travelling with my children on planes would be hell on earth, but I have to say it's not that bad. The people who really suffer are the other passengers who get stressed out just realising there are going to be children on board with them. The reality is that they travel really well, providing I take the obligatory colouring pens and paper and the Game Boy. Then all is as quiet as you can expect it to be with two small children in a confined space.

'I think I've learned two main things about travelling with my children. The first is not to get stressed about it – what's the point? The second, that my daughter is destined to be a lavatory attendant when she grows up. "I want a wee" is all we ever hear. The other thing that has changed is not so much how we get there, but where we are going to go to. Before it was India, the Dominican Republic, Africa. Today it's Majorca and Cyprus. I've even been on a week-long caravan holiday in Great Yarmouth! We can't go anywhere nowadays without a Kids Club. It's become the first priority when booking any holiday. The strange thing is that the kids hate them when we get there but I have to do it for my own reassurance.'

Lucy, thirty-six, mother of Johnny, eight, and Vanda, four

'The same thing happens with your car as with almost everything else in your life. It gets bigger and it gets trashed. Over time I have just had to come to accept that my son has to, and will probably always, customise his area of the car with stickers and all manner of food crap carefully ground into the upholstery. Overall, I think sticky is the best way to describe our car. You can't actually touch anything without sticking to it. And of course, the other great joy about car travel with my child is that when I leap out to post something in the letterbox, when I get back I am guaranteed to die of a heart attack as he has turned on the hazards, the indicators, the windscreen wipers and the radio full blast. He is a constant source of surprise and wonder!

'As for plane travel, I gave up after one trip. I'm saving that little treat until he's older. Frankly, it was enough to put anyone off. We'd managed to get the bulkhead seats so were thrilled with the extra space before realising that this was the type of plane with one giant TV screen – right in front of us. Having fed my son and almost got him to sleep the big feature blasted into life. *Jurassic Park Two*. A film that begins with dinosaurs eating a child. What could be more perfect?! The whole flight was then spent walking up and down the aisles trying to shield his face from it and get him back to sleep whilst he twisted and turned around. Each time we passed from cabin to cabin – there it was again! Who the heck wants to see dinosaurs eat children? After six or seven hours on a plane with him though, I can only conclude it is an option! The trip ended on a really high note, as he vomited all over me upon landing, whilst the stewardess could only pass me small cocktail napkins from her strapped position. The nightmare was finally complete when collecting the hire car. I complained that it was filthy, only to be met with a look of complete disdain. "Oh really," said the man behind the counter, looking me up and down. He clearly had no kids.

'Destinations are another treat too. I remember St Lucia, little weekends away in spa-like hotels, with waiters in white making little drinks, being able to read the Sunday papers. Now other people get the Sunday papers and the little drinks while I'm out playing on the lawn with my child so he won't disturb them! Destinations? From St Lucia to Grandma's basically.'

Jo, thirty-three, mother of Luke, three

'My life is over. From a Mini when we were a couple, to a Fiesta with just one child. An Astra with two and now a Granada for three. And is it filthy? Oh, yes. The other thing that's really changed is where we go to now, particularly on holiday. Whereas it could have been the Caribbean, now it's Spain, and wherever we go there has to be Kids Club. The other thing I've started doing, as bad as it may be, is to take my kids out of school for holidays. I just couldn't stand the thought of a holiday during the school ones. That would be just too many children and I've already got enough of my own, thanks. The one good thing about travelling with my kids, though, is that it doesn't matter how we're travelling or where we're going they all sleep, all of the way and I don't have to worry about them for hours. Perhaps we should holiday on the move.'

Grace, thirty-eight, mother of Jessica, nine, Tabitha, seven, and Graeme, five

'From Porsche 911S 1973 classic to clapped-out VW Passat second-hand, a boring but reliable steed which has been set upon from without and within. It's always full, and at first I used to make some concerted efforts to bring some sense of order to it but now I've really just handed it over to the vagaries of London life and bringing up children. There really is no other way. As for where I take my children, it doesn't seem to matter where we go it is always a logistical nightmare. I may moan about the Passat but at least now we can avoid public transport. A good thing, particularly after we lost our six-year-old daughter on the Tube. She got on and the doors closed before we were in and off she whizzed into the tunnel. Fortunately she was delivered straight back on a returning train by a kindly guard but it won't be something we'll be trying again. To be honest we never venture more than two hours away. That way our children are good travellers.

We try to ensure minimising any problems with travel by not being too ambitious about it. No long-haul flights or drives for the first five years.'

Anthony, thirty-seven, father of Zoe, six, Addie, five, and Mac, two

'Everything expanded when I had a child, not just my waistline, and we even ended up getting a bigger car so the buggy and all the crap fitted in more easily and also so my son couldn't travel everywhere with his feet wedged permanently in my back. Why do they do that? It became a family thing to work out whose turn it was to have him sitting behind them before we set off anywhere. Gone too are the days of a quick Hoover. These days we have to remove all the seats to get rid of stray Smarties and other matter that lurks beneath. And why doesn't sand ever come out? What special properties does it have that ensures a visit to the beach two years ago will linger on in your car for time immemorial? Add to that the joys, or rather fallout, of a McDonald drive-thru and you've got a recipe for disaster along with a guarantee that every car clear-out is a real treat.

'Whether it's the car, plane or train travel these days we can't go anywhere without pens, paper, toys, Game Boy . . . Fenegan is also very good. But in reality I suppose we just pray that he sleeps without drugs and if he doesn't oblige we just patronise him and humour him generally until we arrive. I just dread the day when he can tell the time and no longer believes my constant response of "Just ten more minutes," to his staggeringly repetitive, "Are we nearly there yet?" Roll on the day when all cars come with a video screen fitted in the back as standard – it's my only hope.

'As far as destinations are concerned I can only suggest that if you're going to go out, pick your place. Go Italian on the whole. As far as other members of the public are concerned I'm afraid they really ought just to get on with it. Most of us at least attempt to modify our children's behaviour. We don't deliberately come out to annoy, but nor should we hide at home for fear of doing so.'

Kate, forty-three, mother of Will, six

'We have managed not to concede in any way at all as far as our car is concerned. My husband loves driving and it's the one area where he refuses to compromise. Our daughter sits in the front and I've become a contortionist and sit in the back – which is roughly big enough for a five-year-old. When she's older we're intending to keep the car but we will be restricted to one item of hand luggage only. I'll take my bag and she can take her teddy.'

Sonia, thirty-three, mother of Tatiana, three

'As for cars, having two kids is not much change from one. You will already in any case have dispensed with your old banger or your boy racer during your partner's first gestation period, and made the transition to sensible family saloon. But having got your Vauxhall Vectra, you now need a vasectomy. Because any more than two kids and even your "family" car will be too small. It's get a vasectomy or get a minibus.

'In any event, it's best never to go anywhere *en famille, en voiture*. Since the rigmarole of coaxing your passengers into the vehicle, fixing them securely in their car seats, and making sure you've remembered everything you could possibly need for the two-mile journey to Asda is a logistical effort on a par with NASA sending a manned mission to Mars.

'If you are tempted out, however, and you have a car stereo, remember to rip it out before you set off. You'll never hear Mozart or the Doors again in any case and "Old Macdonald had a Farm" tends to pall a bit after the zillionth "ee aye ee aye oh".

'I hear of some brave but lunatic souls driving to the south of France with two kids, aged two and nought. Personally I'd sooner drive to hell and in a hand cart – or a double buggy. The thought of hundreds of miles of "Old Macdonald", "Wheels on the Bus", or "Polly had a Dolly", interrupted by only two breast-feed stops is just too awful to contemplate. Remember, in any case, that a holiday with two young infants is really only an opportunity to change nappies and wipe up sick in unfamiliar and more challenging surroundings.

'So no travel, but nights out? This one's simple. There are none. Well, not proper ones. Having two kids as opposed to one doesn't radically alter things – it just cranks up the impossibility factor another notch. Because should you manage to find a babysitter who a) costs less than the annual GDP of Kuwait and b) is better with kids than King Herod you've still got double the chance that it will all go horribly pear-shaped and you'll get the call to rush home before the waiter's even shown you the menu.'

With grateful thanks to Mark Whitaker. Reproduced from WIPE *magazine*

'Learned helplessness. It's the only answer. I have three children and absolutely refuse to learn to drive. That way any substantial trips that may involve transporting children or carrying stuff have to involve another adult – childcare problem solved. Also, when making longer car journeys I insist we play Handel because the children love it and think it's brave knight music and on days when they're not so keen we can just turn it up full volume and not even hear the protestations too much! These days we've given up on wonderful romantic trips, we now just want gardens that are enclosed and not covered in dog s***. Uncivilised places that'll accept uncivilised people generally.

'The other great nightmare of course is going out to eat. When your children eventually stop running riot for long enough for you to catch them you then discover the restaurant only has highchairs without straps so you can spend the rest of the meal trying to prevent your offspring from launching themselves to the floor at high velocity. But that's nothing compared to the embarrassment of visiting friends for lunch and having to attach your clip-on highchair to their best antique table – that's always a good moment out with your children, one when you just wish you hadn't bothered after all. Then there are open windows and water features in gardens. Treats I never even realised lay in store.

'And it's almost guaranteed that when you are going somewhere important and have a small child with you that they will vomit on you just before you get out of the car.

'It's probably less stressful to stay at home but the price

for that is insanity. So my decision is to take my life, and those of all those we will come into contact with, into both hands and get out there.

'One final word of caution: be careful not only of where you go, but also who you choose to go with.'

Fiona, thirty-four, mother of Patrick, five, William, three, and Rose, one

What more can I say? Don't leave the house with a small child unless utterly compelled by imminent starvation or the pressing need for other adult company. And if you must go forth allow yourself ample time for packing the suitcase-full of goodies you will imagine you require for even the most modest journey.

Me? I'm a reformed character. Why only this morning I managed to close my vast handbag for the first time in several years and to get into the car without first having to remove an assortment of toys, lolly sticks and other unidentifiable debris from the seat. My son was none too happy, but he'll adjust given time.

Wipe wisdom

- Take less but keep the car. At least that way you know you can row in private.
- Shop on the Internet to counteract all supermarket kid problems.
- Ride the rollercoaster.

12

The Education Maze

Time to do your homework

As a small child I had no idea how keen my mother was for me to sit or speak for the first time. Indeed, if I had I might have used it to my own advantage, so in many ways I'm glad that my son is blissfully unaware of my eagle eye watching every step of his growth. While personal and professional achievements used to be something I kept a half-hearted eye on, now I'm a parent I have to confess to a far greater obsession with reaching developmental milestones, or, rather, my son reaching them and me silently, but somewhat smugly, breathing a sigh of relief. And I use the word silently advisedly. What can be worse than an outspoken proud parent? They're boring in the extreme and have been known to induce violent urges in the best of us.

But in addition what is 'normal' anyway? A cycle on a washing machine, as far as I'm aware. So should I really care whether my son achieves according to someone else's targets, or would it be better to trust a little more to luck and nature and have faith that he'll grow up (eventually) relatively balanced, able to walk in a straight line, hearing perfectly, albeit selectively, and with a range of social skills?

The lure of competition

I'd love to claim that I'm totally relaxed about developmental milestones and about how my child is doing in comparison to his peers, but these days, alongside juggling my career, friendships and life in general, I constantly carry the nagging concerns about how he's progressing. Should I be pushing him more, or less, or somewhere in between? I don't want to be a pushy mother (who, me?) but I'm only human and I do look out for every goal and achievement. And not just those of my own little darling. It's good to know what the competition is up to. After all, knowing where the others are at helps me to develop my paranoia about my son's ability quite nicely, thank you.

'Who did you play with at school today?' I ask. But am I really interested or am I just checking that his social interaction is developing nicely and that he's mixing with the brightest children in his class? 'What did you learn at school today?' When his reply is, 'I can't remember,' it only adds fuel to my panic. Is he just tired after a day at school? Is he merely focusing on what he's doing now that he's at home? Or has he got short-term memory problems and should I whisk him off to the local educational psychologist before returning home to burn the fish fingers as I interrogate him still further?

And on top of all the angst his development produces in me, not to mention the ferocious competitiveness I struggle ineffectually to stem, I am seriously worried about my own developmental milestones, which seem to have regressed in direct proportion to his progress. While he was developing hand-eye coordination the truth was I found myself losing mine. Night after night of sleep deprivation and the new-found necessity to multitask at all times saw nicely to that. And while he developed the ability to speak I was waving goodbye to that too. Apart from my new-found inability to string a sentence together I found I had little or no conversation anyway, due to the astonishing lack of anything in my life apart from parenthood and domesticity. So while his social skills developed I had to face mine falling apart. I reached my own personal developmental all-time low when I arrived in a world of 'Ooh, look. Big red bus.'

I remember going for a job interview when my son was just learning to speak and when asked what I could bring to the position I was only just awake enough to stop a short but stunning rendition of 'Postman Pat and his Black and White Cat' escaping from my lips. Emergency action was called for and with the help of a twice-weekly babysitter I escaped, if only to see a friend or read the papers over fish and chips, and began to claw my way slowly back to relative sanity and conversational skills.

The fact is that I haven't yet met a parent who isn't obsessed with their child's developmental milestones and who doesn't eye up other people's children and their progress on the quiet. Underneath we're all horribly competitive and desperate for our children to achieve their full potential. To which end we're busy piling the pressure on to them as well as ourselves.

'I really needed to know where each of my children were along the line, all the time. I was desperately concerned that they should arrive at each target on time. I felt under a huge amount of pressure, looking back on it, and if they weren't all exactly average I worried myself sick. And if any of them was ahead in any area I was "Smug Mum" and I'm ashamed to say that I boasted to anyone and everyone foolish enough to hang around long enough for me to get started.'

Vanessa, forty-one, mother of Robbie, thirteen, Mark, ten, and Simone, six

'I was totally, totally paranoid. Every time my son cried I'd leap up and announce, "He's teething, you know." He was teething from birth, it's just that it took a year for the first one to come through! I compared him to other children his age constantly and was horrendously smug when he was the first one to sit unaided at the local mother and baby coffee morning. It made up for how inadequate I'd always felt there. God, how embarrassing.'

Ruth, thirty-seven, mother of Joshua, five

'So far I haven't got stressed about whether our daughter reaches targets on time. As long as she's normal and healthy I'm happy. In truth, though, as her father will obviously expect her to be President of America before she's twelve things could get a little tricky. Perhaps it's best to say that we'll be just fine with developmental milestones so long as she's normal and happy and first in everything.'

Anna, thirty-four, mother of Chloe, one

Pack your satchel . . .

Finally, after four or five short years of their lives, and what may well feel like forty or fifty to us, children reach school age. While at this stage your life stands the vaguest chance of returning to a state of equilibrium, first we have to figure out where they're going to go to nursery and which infant school would best suit their own, oh so individual needs.

That's all before even considering how on earth you're going to get to work and back again when you only drop them off at ten past nine and need to be back some six hours later. And, oh, yes, then there are the holidays, for them that is, not you! I had no idea what I should be looking for in a nursery or school other than what common sense dictated: good results, happy children and a strong commitment to fair treatment and equality alongside zero tolerance of bullying. I felt inadequate in the extreme, but so far our experience of the local church nursery and infant school has been wonderful.

Despite this I am still weighed down with guilt and questions. Guilt at the fact that as a financially scuppered, single mother I simply can't offer my son the private education and choices that were so generously bestowed upon me as a child. And questions such as: does he receive enough stimulation? Will he have enough motivation to do well? Is there enough praise? Is he pushed too much, too young? Does he suffer separation anxiety or, in real language, does he miss me? And how do I cope with my own separation anxiety?

At the end of the day, private or state, wherever I had

chosen, I expect I would have experienced all of the above and more. And today, having made a decision, despite his being perfectly happy, I still spend a lot of my day panicking on his behalf and desperately disciplining myself not to transfer my own fears and experience of the education system on to him. His might well be different – I can but hope! My own peers were a scary bunch and, although I don't always see it, perhaps I was too, in my own way.

Will his friendships be strong and reliable? I find myself wondering. Will they be the ones I would choose for him? Will he be bullied? Will he be true to himself? I find myself hanging on to the words of Samuel Johnson: 'Almost every man wastes part of his life attempting to display qualities which he does not possess.' Wise words and my son will be no exception.

'The school was pretty, very pretty. Pretty uniforms, pretty children, pretty classrooms, and very pretty star charts. There were charts for everything. Good work and bad. Bad behaviour and good. Indeed one felt that one only had to move and a merit certificate or star would be eagerly awarded.

'I realised this would not be the right school for my son when a dull and horsy Sloane showed us the hothouse room. My two-year-old screeched "No" and ran out immediately. Very wise, I thought, given that this was the room where they took the very bright or the very slow to hothouse. Who wants to be either? I thought, and one certainly wouldn't want to be hot-housed by a horsy Sloane. My overriding impression was that while learning here may be tidy it would also certainly be dull.

'We watched the four-year-olds in the French class. "*Bleu*" they chanted as a twitty, floral-clad French teacher held up a picture of a blue balloon. Where were the space rockets, the chatter of hungry minds and where were the enthusiastic and bright-eyed teachers?

'Identical rows of spacemen immediately aroused my suspicions at the next school I visited. At least they were doing spacemen, but identical ones? One classroom consisted of a table and chairs, neatly stacked shelves and a reading corner. Very anal. A group of five children sat obediently doing number work. The atmosphere was so repressive that I felt like pulling my pants down and I'm not three! No water, no sand, no dough, no fun.

'"Would you like to come to this school?" the owner of this establishment asked my son. "No," he replied. She forced a smile, I made myself do the same and my son scowled. He had definitely failed his entrance examination. "I didn't like it," he told me after we'd left. "No," I replied. "Neither did I." I knew that we had to find a school where I could say, with complete conviction, "Wow, you're going to your first day at school, how exciting."

'Having wearily tramped around many private establishments I started on the state school system. But I felt anxious as I approached the state nursery recommended by a friend. It was my last hope, and I didn't hold out much, having seen what was on offer so far. We trooped down the dark staircase and into educational paradise. No identical spacemen here, but creative individualistic expression everywhere. A number table overflowed with every kind of puzzle, game and counter. A home corner with silver shoes and fireman outfits. A construction area with every kind of brick and building block. Dinosaurs in the science area, books everywhere, paint, dough, sand and tiny drawers stuffed with colours and textures for collage. Play outside included a climbing frame, bikes, scooters, hoops, balls, basketball nets, sandpit and paddling pool.

'Children busied themselves everywhere, genuinely filling the school's philosophy of learning through play at this early stage of their educational lives. I knew this would be the right place for my bright, intensive and lively three-year-old. Most impressive and important of all was the wisdom and sensitivity of the school headmistress. Nothing was going to be forced here, no knowledge stuffed unwanted into little minds. Here their natural intelligence could blossom in this stimulating environment, their talents discovered and interests found.

'"I don't want to go home," sobbed my son and my fifteen-month-old lay on the floor and had a tantrum. Unfazed by all this emotion the head assured my son that she would see him soon. "Wow, how exciting. You're starting school," I could finally declare.

'The first week was a total nightmare. My son cried because he didn't want me to leave him, my toddler cried because he wanted to be left, my baby cried because I'd left him with the nanny and I felt like crying too because my hormones were all over the place.

'Worst of all was that well-known curse of motherhood. Guilt. I was guilty I hadn't prepared my son more for this moment of separation. Guilty I hadn't made him feel secure enough to feel he could cope without me. Guilty that . . . guilty about everything.

'"Assure him you understand how he feels," a psychotherapist friend advised. "It's a perfectly healthy response to being left," she told me. Encouraged by her words I stopped saying, "You'll be fine," and followed her advice. The very next day he skipped off enthusiastically and has never looked back since.'

Jane, thirty-six, mother of James, four, Bob, three, and Peter, one

'We chose our children's nursery and primary school purely because they were the best ones in the area and thankfully the closest too. The education they get is brilliant but it's come at a price. There's no playground at the school to speak of and as a result the kids don't really get to run around, which also means they're not as exhausted at the end of the day as I would like them to be. Having said that, the school is great.

'I would never send them anywhere that wasn't a church school because at the end of the day even if they choose not to be religious when they grow up I think it will have given them a certain set of values that are important. Also they are required to wear a uniform and that matters to me a great deal too. There's nothing worse in my mind than seeing a load of scruffy kids whose parents are all feeling the pressure of decking them out in the latest fashions. This way nobody's different or feels less than the others. It doesn't matter if you have 2p or two thousand in your purse, nobody knows. The only thing I'd change is the playground situation; other than that they've got religion, a uniform and great results. What more could we ask for?

'I've also become really active in the PTA. As much as I might loathe it and feel I don't have the time to spare, at the end of the day they're my kids and that means it's my responsibility to go and check out what's going on at the school and have my say. We can agree and disagree but at least I feel I'm taking an active interest and playing an active role in a major part of their lives.

'Homework is a real headache. I'm very, very strict indeed when it comes to that because otherwise we have horrendous Sunday nights each week. These days I make my son sit down on Friday when he comes in from school and get it over with however much he might protest. I just find it hard to believe that it hasn't driven me back to smoking again.

'On top of school we also do loads of extra-curricular activities. Cubs, swimming, football and stage school. Mainly, I think, because I did when I was little and loved it. On top of that it means that he gets away from his own environment. He's not tied constantly to our home and it broadens his horizons. Finally, they're great because he loves them and that means they are a privilege that can be removed if he's repeatedly naughty. That as an overhanging threat seems to help keep the tantrums under control.'

Elizabeth, thirty-six, mother of Todd, seven

'We haven't got there yet. But already the pressure is on. Living in London makes the whole schools business ridiculous. The days when kids simply went to the nearest school are long gone. Now they commute. We live barely a netball throw from our nearest primary school and yet are sweating that the nearest available place for Daisy may be at a school on the dark side of the moon. And what if she DOES get in? And Jack doesn't? Do we all up sticks? I want my kids to go to school – but not if it means walking to Australia. The thought of bundling them both into a Range Rover every morning to drive them to a seat of learning that's light years away from where we live fills me with gloom.'

With grateful thanks to Mark Whitaker, radio presenter and writer.

Reproduced from WIPE *magazine*

'Where to send our son to school was an agonising decision that fed all known neuroses to a vast degree. We applied to about sixteen schools and then when we were accepted by the three best ones it became an impossible situation and I ended up going to see an educational consultant. They must just love people like us: indecisive and desperate for the best for our children. There's this awful middle-class fear that I get stuck into. I always said I wouldn't get competitive and that all I wanted was a good school where he would be happy. By the time he was four I had decided that education mattered more than anything in the world and that he had to get in to a brilliant nursery in order to guarantee his safe passage to Oxford in later years.

'Once in a good nursery the next agonising decision on the path to Oxford was the primary school. That's when it got really tough. On top of that, once we'd made our final decision I discovered, with horror, that all the other mothers seemed to know each other and I couldn't work out how! All my insecurities flashed up on to my huge internal Imax cinema of my mind. They all had thin thighs, they all had . . . I felt as an American mother in England that I'd missed some subtle clothing clues along the way and was convinced if I didn't dress right and do everything else right my son would suffer at school as a result. If I get this wrong, I told myself, he'll suffer, he'll pay the price. The whole thing was a nightmare, from school decision to dress code. I just couldn't get it right.'

Cheryl, thirty-two, mother of Kevin, six

'I really wanted a very strict disciplinary school, preferably a church one, not because we are religious maniacs but because I really believe that they would get better values because of it.

'Extra-curricular activities – with three children they're a logistical nightmare but a must. They get them out of my face and wear them out into the bargain. What more could a mother ask for?'

Jana, forty, mother of Etta, ten, Minty, eight, and Peta, six

'Education. Great because the school gets good results and the children get good discipline. Bad because we never have our hands out of our pockets. Good because he's making progress. Bad because homework is a stressful nightmare, resulting in everyone in tears.

'Extra-curricular activities. Good because they fill that graveyard shift between four p.m. and eight p.m. Bad because my hand's back in my pocket again, and now I run a taxi service too.'

Sonia, thirty-nine, mother of Kirsty, ten, and Lucy, seven

Parents' evenings

One huge highlight for me of my son entering the world of education is the fact that I now get the opportunity to re-enter it myself in the form of parents' evenings. Only this time I get to be the grown-up instead of the continuously berated child. And the experience does not disappoint. But do I really understand a word they are saying to me? Or indeed believe them? Is this my child they're talking about? And do they recognise his clearly genius potential?

> 'The worst aspect of education has to be the parents' evenings where I don't even recognise the child they're talking about. They're also complete chaos and take four hours to negotiate which I could well do without, particularly when I don't feel I've learned anything of value at the end of it anyway. But there you go, we have to do it.'
>
> *Mel, thirty-five, mother of Joanna, seven, and Katie, five*

> 'We were just driven by the best schools available locally and became determined to get them into one of them. Fortunately they're subsidised too. Parents' evenings I loathe. I do go to them but they just leave me feeling old and sad and whilst I'm not sure I believe a word they're saying, the good side is that I do feel it's an opportunity to have my say and make a small difference, perhaps, to my children's education.'
>
> *Anthony, thirty-seven, father of Michael, nine, and William, six*

Many parents leave parents' evenings none the wiser about their children's progress. What is it that teachers are on about? For the definitive insider's guide, read on, as Nicholas Corder, author and former teacher, spills the beans;

'Jimmy is making good progress': your child is nondescript. There are thirty-three children in his class and I only have them for an hour a week. I don't know if your child is the quiet mousy pudding, the quiet blonde pudding or the quiet dark pudding. Rest assured that your child is a pudding.

'I'll look into it for you': no, I won't. Please go away. The longer you hover around here, the longer it is before I can get in the pub and sink a few pints.

'Tim is making fair progress': no, he isn't. In teacher-speak 'good' equals 'none'. 'Fair' means he is going backwards.

'Adrian reads widely': Adrian runs a pornography ring.

'Mark is mature for his years': Mark has reached puberty ahead of his classmates. He now spends most of his time pushing the smaller children about.

'Mark must learn to be more generous to his smaller classmates': okay, so we ignored it when he was just pushing them about, but now he has a full-scale protection racket going.

'Tim is always happy for a change of air': he smokes. Possibly not just tobacco.

'Luke always helps the girls in the class': he is forever twanging bra straps and will pick up anything dropped on the floor just so as to get a flash at their knickers.

'Nigel struggles with some of the harder concepts': no, he doesn't. He struggles with some of the easier concepts. In fact, he has no concept at all.

'Sam may be dyslexic': Sam isn't dyslexic at all. Remember there are two forms of dyslexia. The first is genuine, the second is non-existent. Sam's got the second sort. He just never reads anything, so now he is struggling to keep up. Doesn't dyslexia sound a whole lot better than illiterate? It excuses both me as his teacher, you as his parents, and Sam for the idle, lame-brain that he is. It will also provide some dyslexia outfit with a fat fee to assess him. We all win on this one.

'Harry is always willing in class': yes, willing to interrupt, willing to talk back, willing to disrupt, swear, talk about anything but the subject in hand.

'Jack needs to show more restraint from time to time': so does the teacher. In fact, if Jack makes one more stupid remark about the size of women's breasts, teacher will have to show enough restraint not to strangle him with his bare hands. And don't think it's just confined to the boys. Girls can be just as problematic – especially if they're called Samantha.

'Samantha is socially aware': Samantha is sexually active.

'Samantha is very active': Samantha is sexually active.

'Samantha is such a generous girl': Samantha likes to bestow sexual favours on some of the older boys.

'Samantha is a pragmatic child': she also charges money.

'Samantha is a chip off the old block': I hear her mother's anybody's for the price of a lager top.

'Samantha is such an adventurous child': Samantha is a total headbanger. We had to get the fire brigade to coax her off the sports hall roof. Luckily one of Mr Jones's old chemistry students is now in charge of Blue Watch, so it didn't make the local paper.

'Samantha seems to have settled down a little recently: Samantha was rather taken with the fireman who helped her down off the sports hall roof.

'Samantha often fails to distinguish between fact and fiction': just like her teacher really.

With grateful thanks to Nicholas Corder. Reproduced from *WIPE* magazine

So the next time you find yourself in your child's school, facing the bleak, stuffy prospect of a parents' evening, spare a thought for the poor teachers. After all, most of them are racking their brains to think of some way of being economical with the truth.

Hidden extras

What I have also learned is that along with my son starting school comes the chance to suffer extreme humiliation and embarrassment at the hands of my innocent child. Pre-school, and school itself, are where the family laundry is gently washed and hung on public display for the entire class and playground to see, and my son certainly hasn't let me down on that one. Some of his greatest achievements to date have been announcing his mother's membership to both the RAC and AA, only the latter not having anything to do with cars, before describing in graphic detail and with enormous embellishments what he understood it to be, alongside the things he most loves about me. Apparently that I am bonkers, long and friendly and have a tattoo. Marvellous.

And if that wasn't enough, after extricating my wounded and blushing pride from the playground, following a lengthy discussion with the headmaster on the subject of my son's disclosures at the end of each day, I apparently get to do homework too. Yippee. Not to mention, a real bonus this, an assortment of extra-curricular activities. Just how good does life get? Strangely I'd been labouring under the illusion that school finished at three thirty and that it was him in attendance, not me. Just how wrong could I be?

Extra-curricular activities! A whole wealth of opportunities lay in wait, which, while they sound as though they're marvellous for your child, regularly prove less than great for the grown-ups. All too often it appears to involve standing around on the sidelines of a cold and wet football pitch for hours on end, an afternoon not dissimilar to my own, this very day. And tomorrow should prove to be just as good. A mission hall in the company of Brown Beaver surrounded by all her 'busy little beavers' never ceases to leave me doubled up and usually results in my leaving the hall to collapse in the privacy of my car and await the return of my very own small, but eager, beaver and his shiny woggle. Call me juvenile but could they not have chosen an animal with a different name?

'Typical conversation in the kids' shoes department between me – clutching ticket number 53 and fast losing the will to live – and a woman (still in that blissful stage of parenthood ungoverned by anything as tedious as timetables and name tags) buying off-the-peg slippers for her pre-school toddler.

'Her: "When do your three go back to school?"

'Me: "Next Wednesday."

'"I bet you can't wait for life to get back to normal?" she asks with the ignorant air of one who has just potty-trained her two-year-old and assumes she has very few child-rearing challenges left to conquer. I don't have the heart to frighten her. Like many mothers before me I fail to warn her of the impending homework fatwah that is about to hit and which will alter life as she knows it for ever.

'For sadly, life does not "get back to normal" when you send your children to full-time school – that is the vile myth perpetuated by teachers, and parents who have no life and don't work. If you work and aspire to a social life marginally more exciting than attending PTA meetings you are buggered big-time.

'Freedom all but disappears during term-time. Oh, the pressure starts out slowly enough when you first pick up your five-year-old and her reading folder. She's so thrilled to be entrusted with a task and you're so brimming with pride she's been separated from you and made it through the day, you're lulled into a false sense of security. It's only six weeks into the term, when you're burning the dinner, the baby's got savage colic and your best friend's on the telephone wanting to tell you about sex with a toy boy, that you get the first inkling of what it's like to be under house arrest.

'"I'm going to read up to page twenty-nine tonight," announces Molly, "so I'll be better than Etta." And by Jove she does read up to page twenty-nine. And it takes an hour. And you have to concentrate. And cajole and correct and listen to what happens when Peter gets on the bus, gets off the bus, drives the bus and go through the whole boring story again when Jane decides she wants to get on the bus too. But homework is still new and she's only been at big school for six weeks and is already on Green level and the fatwah hasn't really altered your life – yet.

'But wait until they're eight. Wait until you've got one child in Junior and two in Senior. Wait until the projects kick in. Wait until the folder comes home with a piece of A4 instructing your daughter to "Make a Viking ship over the weekend." Imagine that is the weekend you are going to visit friends in Oxford for Sunday lunch, you've got a dinner party for eight on Friday night, your irritable bowel syndrome is playing up and your husband is away working. You try making a Viking ship over the weekend that is good enough for your child, who would only be satisfied if David Linley himself had spent forty-eight hours toiling in his workshop in Dorset.

'Kids today have progressed from *Blue Peter*-style handiwork. They want the Full Monty. No painted loo rolls for them. They have gone off homework, but are competitive enough to want to impress the offspring of foreign parents, who always remain slightly in awe of the English school system. These goodie-goodie parents go into project overdrive. They obviously cancel their weekend arrangements, drug themselves up to combat crippling stomach ache and airlift their husbands back home. They appear on Monday morning proudly bearing the fruits of their efforts, their child smugly trotting alongside, secure in the knowledge they're about to get an A for their meticulously scaled model which is the result of three trips to Homebase, a long-distance telephone call to a godfather who happens to be in the Marines and a nasty moment in Casualty when Daddy caught his thumb in the electric sander.

'Your child, meanwhile, is in a blind, sulking fury, clutching an old cereal packet which you've viciously hacked into a banana-shaped canoe and stuck toothpicks into the base. You're stressed, splattered with poster paint and late with a deadline. This is the fourth attempt at making the damn thing stick and most of Sunday afternoon was spent arguing with your twelve-year-old about a Shakespearean play you haven't read with a child who presumably has, but needs help recalling a single character other than Leonardo di Caprio.

'"Darling," you say as your child eyes up an American mother who is handing over a Martha Stewart cake swimming in a sea of blue icing, replete with sugared Vikings she had sent over from Texas having ordered them off the Internet last term, "Mrs King will like yours more because she'll realise you did it all by yourself." But Molly's not convinced. Especially when she fails to get a star.

'Next weekend is worse. The project is endangered species and Mrs American has already downloaded an entire Amazon forest of information for little Grace, while you've done nothing except pick up a Dorling Kindersley book of elephants and can't truthfully remember whether it's the African or the Indian ones that gave up their lives to make that rather pretty ivory box you've got in the drawing room.

'You have now turned into Hitler over the homework. The fatwah has taken over completely. You dread opening the homework diary even more than brown envelopes from the Inland Revenue. The halcyon days of motherhood are over. You are a nagging witch, too knackered with supervising homework to go out on school nights unless it's to W.H. Smith's where you give your swipe card a workout by buying endless inks, erasers, pencils and highlighters. Schools have upped the ante. It's no longer enough to be a parent, you're expected to be a teacher too.

'The trouble is, times have changed and along with New Labour came New Maths. New Maths requires Nurofen and a brain as refined as Stephen Hawkings'. Physics and chemistry are mercifully out of the equation completely as I never did them in my day, so I've got the pink ticket and am not considered worth asking for help. In my day we learned tame poems about owls and were taught how to make inedible flapjacks. I don't remember pressure being a part of my childhood. I just remember doing twenty minutes' history on Thursday evenings whilst watching *Top of the Pops*.

> 'So as term goes on and time goes by I write increasingly furious notes to various teachers. I make up excuses about why the geography didn't get finished. It didn't get finished because I had better things to do with my life than supervise an exhausted child who doesn't just want me to "help" at the end of a long school day, she wants me to cancel an evening at the theatre in order to trace a map of the world with all the continents clearly marked, and I haven't got the time or the energy. If I'm being completely honest, I don't really have the inclination either.
>
> 'Am I glad they're going back to school on Wednesday? Are you out of your mind? I'm dreading it. I love every split second of the holidays. Believe it or not, I love being a mother, and it's infinitely more rewarding than trying to be an unqualified teacher. The fatwah of homework is more tedious than reading a book by Salman Rushdie and just as interminable.'
>
> *With grateful thanks to Sarah Standing. Reproduced from* WIPE *magazine*

So much to look forward to. So much to learn. So much to pack in to just fourteen short years at school.

And that's just us parents.

Makes you want to have another baby this very moment, doesn't it?

Wipe wisdom

- Trust your own judgement when it comes to developmental milestones. Intuition's there for a reason and parents tend to know their children best.

- Be very, very careful what you tell your child about your private life. Only mention things you'd like the entire teaching staff and playground to know by three thirty tomorrow.

- Prepare yourself for parents' evenings with a few stiff drinks and arrive armed with a photo of your child in order to jog his teacher's memory.

- Lay down the law about homework. You'll only do it in exchange for your child's solemn promise not to wake you up on Sunday mornings or send the babysitter home in tears again.

13

You've Got a Ramp, What More Do You Want?

What happens when your child has special needs?

'Yes, I'll have a baby at around thirty. We'll want some time together first, but it's probably sensible to start a family around then. After all we still want to be young enough to kick a football around the park.'

So that'll be two egg-fried rice, one rogan josh, two chicken masalas and a baby to go please. If only it were that simple. A baby to order. Where does this naïve belief come from that we can just have a child as and when it suits us? When the reality is often unplanned, unexpected, faster, or, indeed, much slower, than we had predicted.

And if we do manage to conceive, be it accidentally, haphazardly or after months of the gynaecological dentistry otherwise known as IVF, we immediately proceed to career headlong into life's next little myth that everything in the garden will be rosy.

'Mother and baby are doing well.' The waiting masses embrace and the baby's head is well and truly soaked. After all, we've not needed an amniocentesis or been told to prepare for the worst, negotiating the agonising decisions that then need to be taken. All will be well. We're in safe hands.

Surely the worst that can happen at this final furlong are a few tears, the odd scream, excruciating pain and several stitches later the memory will miraculously evaporate and a perfect family will be made.

Yet although around 300,000 children are born each year in the UK complete with the proverbial rosy cheeks, one in fifty are born with a degree of abnormality. I, like so many others, certainly hadn't planned on my child being one of this minority. Like everyone else I expected that at the end of nine long uncomfortable months we'd have a healthy, rosy-cheeked baby. How wrong I was. At six months old my child became ill with what proved to be long-term health difficulties and the world of parenthood became even more of a practical and emotional minefield than it had been before. And while having my son fulfilled my wildest dreams, it also took me well beyond my wildest nightmares.

Coming to terms with disability

When facing the news that their child has problems it is inevitable that parents will respond in numerous different ways. Collapsing now, later or intermittently are all valid responses. Just as are anger, denial and fear. Be prepared that the long road to acceptance of your child's disability will be an arduous one. If the illness is immediately identifiable the upside is that you can arm yourself with knowledge and relevant support groups. The downside is that you run the risk of imposing accepted restrictions on your child's potential development.

A diagnosis that is not so obvious is clearly harrowing in another way. The advantage to be remembered in such cases is that no one can place a limit on your child's future. We lived for a very long time without a clear diagnosis, before coming to understand what a relatively rare condition my son has, and it was undoubtedly a difficult time, full of fear and dread, masked by an intermittently brave face.

Whatever the case, start to think of yourself as an expert on your child's health. The reality is that you are in the best position to help your child. I trusted my instincts when it came to identifying the right specialists to back up my hunches. It often meant travelling across vast expanses of the country, with small child in tow. But it was worth it. Traditionally we parents meekly agree with the professionals, but while I had to work alongside the medics, being well-informed was not only my responsibility, it was also extremely empowering and helped my own wellbeing.

If this is the scenario that touches your lives, then, with or without a label, it is vital that, as parents, we make time for ourselves and our children. Following illness and diagnosis, be prepared. Numerous people with endless opinions will inevitably appear and while these can be helpful, or not, don't let them come between you and your child. I made time for the two of us to enjoy each other's company, going at my child's pace and it benefited both of us enormously.

Keeping a record about him also helped from day one.

Factual accounts not only helped the medics and other professionals build a comprehensive picture but making space to write about my own feelings helped me to deal with them on a relatively regular basis.

Johnny was born a little early, but perfect. At six weeks old his parents, like many of us with newborn babies, first children in particular, were concerned that something wasn't quite right. So Johnny was taken off to the GP for professional advice, only to be told he was 'fine'. His parents returned home feeling 'a little silly' as we all do from time to time when worrying about our offspring. The next day, however, his mother followed her gut instinct, left work and returned home immediately. Johnny's mother was in for the first shock of many that were to follow. His nanny said Johnny was asleep but, looking into his cot, his mother found him blue. In Accident and Emergency meningitis was diagnosed. During the following three weeks in hospital Johnny overdosed on an anticonvulsant drug, choked and arrested. After three long weeks of going to hell and back again many times, Johnny appeared to be making a full recovery, but a CT scan showed brain damage likely to lead to physical and/or mental impairment. Johnny is now fifteen with severe spastic quadriplegia, is registered blind and is still mildly epileptic.

Johnny's parents didn't stop to grieve in any way, and when offered counselling they turned it down, focusing all their energies on finding practical measures and taking practical steps to help their son. When he was a baby there was little provision and rehabilitation available for his age group within the community. His parents were offered help to get him into a home. They were horrified and continued in their belief that if they worked hard enough they could make a difference and even 'sort it out'. Every time they saw doctors they were hit head-on with a harsh dose of reality but still they didn't give up hope, looking for every possible resource. They even persuaded special schools for older children to lend them their hydrotherapy pools to use before school started each day.

While they didn't opt for counselling, they drew strength from being around other parents with similar experiences. Keeping 'normal' was Johnny's parents' method of coping. Only in later years, when Johnny became too big to carry easily, did they use special equipment. It's all about making informed decisions, and sticking by what is right for you and your family. As Johnny's mother says: 'Sort out in your head what your approach is to be, what would best suit your family, and then plan what you and your child need and how you are going to get there.'

Dealing with doctors and hospitals

If I've learned little else from this ongoing saga I now know that wherever possible I should deal with myself before I deal with the doctors. Being prepared and in control has a number of advantages and, in situations loaded with emotion and frustration, often produced more constructive results.

In the past I've wanted to scream with frustration but I've learned, through hard-earned experience, that a polite, but firm, tone gets you further. You can always bang your head repeatedly against the nearest wall after leaving the doctor's office. Another tried and tested method of release!

Tears never go down too well during your average discussion with members of the medical fraternity, believe me. I've tried that one too. They look flustered and want to escape, while I simply end up feeling foolish.

So now, when I've had a quick weep in the privacy of my own home, I focus my attention these days on lists, an invaluable tool well worth adopting at an early stage. While visiting our doctor armed with a mountain of information downloaded from the Internet is guaranteed to make even the most tolerant of medics run a mile, being informed and prepared is no bad thing. Experience has taught me that the medical profession appear to work, in general, on the automatic pilot assumption that you have less brain capacity than a flea and live your life just longing to be patronised. Their opening gambit of 'How is Mum today?' is the high point and from there on in it's downhill. So the sooner they know you are capable of spelling a great deal more than your own name, the better.

Every time you meet a new doctor, or even nurse, they will inevitably ask you about your child's history from conception to the present day. By the thirty-fourth time my patience was beginning to wear thin. In the end I typed up a brief two paragraphs summarising everything they could possibly need to know and circulated it to all doctors who held notes on my son with 'To Be Stuck In Front Of File' clearly labelled on each copy.

Finally, despite my general, free-floating frustrations with the whole procedure I try not to forget to thank the medics involved. Partly because they've done their job and need appreciation, just like everyone else, but, also, let's be honest, because it helps.

When taking your child into hospital:

- Make a list on day one of what should happen and when during your stay, for instance when your child's medicine is due. Ensure it happens. Staff are under pressure and you are your child's number one carer.

- Write down events, times and details as a good and reliable record. When you're tired and emotional getting the facts wrong becomes a distinct possibility.

- Look after yourself – right down to the simple basics. Eat at every mealtime, even when you don't feel like it. It keeps you strong and going that much longer.

- Find ways of making yourself comfortable when you are there. Even simple things make a difference.

- Make sure that you have all the support you need in place for when you get home from hospital, and that means from day one.

- Take names and addresses into hospital with you and blast off some calls yourself to be certain everything is in place.

- And finally, get home as quickly as you can. It's cleaner, more comfortable and far more conducive to sanity.

The home front

Be prepared. For while you may assume that as parents you will come to terms with the news of your child's disability and live with it together, an enormous number of relationships end under the stress of severely disabled children. And the staggering statistics are not significantly reduced when a child is diagnosed with less critical but long-term health difficulties.

My own relationship broke down two years into my son's illness, and in retrospect I'm not sure I could have handled the situation leading to the split, and thus prevented it, in any other way. My partner's attitude to the situation was far more positive than my own. I would be lying if I didn't admit that I often feared the worst and I struggled, on a daily basis, with the exhaustion and stress. Years of never sleeping more than two hours at a time are enough to send anyone pretty close to the edge and aren't exactly a recipe for a happy and fulfilling relationship.

Looking back I can see that communication is the key, but, unfortunately, by the end I was unable to communicate how I felt, much less deal with it. And, just as important, we failed to work out a formula for life. Planning strategies for living that will work in your new-found circumstances now seems a vital element if a relationship is to survive.

'Have you ever thought what will happen now?' Johnny's mother clearly remembers asking his father following the news of their son's disability and they have continued to work on being open with each other ever since. 'I feel very lucky,' she says. 'When I was pregnant I thought that he may just be casually along for the ride! But Johnny's father stuck it out and is still very much there fifteen years on.

'Be very kind, and know that he is having as much of a problem dealing with it as you are. It's just normal that men often display it in a less obvious way. Work out how this new situation is going to affect and change your lives and find ways of dealing with it together. Decide whether both, one or neither of you are going to work, and who will be the primary carer. In our case Johnny's dad works and I attempt to leave him as clear as possible during the week to do just that. Remember that in most cases it is the mother who will remain the constant primary carer, particularly if the relationship breaks down. So work out a formula for life. It doesn't have to be set in stone and it will need regular review, but if your relationship is going to be one of the few to survive you need a carefully thought-out baseline at all times.'

More?

The fear of history repeating itself, however unlikely, is no small worry. Someone once told me, in their wisdom, that 'fear' stood for 'f*** everything and run', and when trying to make a decision such as this one it's not an unappealing option. But, should you decide to go ahead and have another child, or if you already have other healthy offspring, the impact on them is not to be underestimated.

Their experience of living with a disabled sibling is,

apparently, not dissimilar to that of their parents, So I suppose I can only assume that if I did ever go down that road again, my next child's experience would often closely parallel my own. What I will endeavour to do, however, is hang on to the fact that, although hard-earned, there are many benefits. Siblings often feel great pride in their brother or sister's abilities and achievements, immense loyalty and are very mature. On the other hand there are a whole range of potential pressures in store for them. There is a very real need for us to ensure that siblings of a disabled child receive the additional support and understanding they need.

- Provide siblings with age-appropriate information; they will have a lifelong need for this.

- Set aside time for each of your children individually.

- Provide opportunities for them to meet other siblings of disabled children.

- Encourage good communication.

- LISTEN to your children; encourage them to talk to you.

- Praise children for the support they give to their disabled sibling.

'We do know that she has had to put up with a lot, and perhaps that would've been easier if she had other siblings apart from just Johnny. Perhaps she would have felt more secure. But this is how it is for our family. Johnny is now away all week at school, so our daughter is the centre of attention then, and I think she would tell you that the tendency is to push her aside a little at weekends when Johnny and all his needs return home. I am ashamed to admit it but there is also a tendency to say 'look at Johnny, there's nothing wrong with you' in response to the inevitable whinges and whines of a child feeling unwell. We even managed not to notice she had glandular fever for a year before I finally caved in and took her to a doctor!

'Thankfully she seems to have benefited from contact with other children in similar situations. She is inordinately proud of all of Johnny's achievements, as the whole family are, but, hey, she's an adolescent. She hates everything from time to time, or even more regularly than that, and if she can hate her mother picking her up at the school gates some days, then she will inevitably hate being the sibling of a disabled child from time to time. But we won't come down on ourselves like a tonne of bricks – we haven't failed. Just done our best and we hope one day she'll find the understanding to forgive us our inadequacies.'

Special needs and the education maze

The pressure we feel under to give our children a good start in life is immense, and I am afraid it's not lessened when your child has special needs. Before anyone pulls me up on this, I am fully aware that all children have special needs, and that differentiation should be provided at all stages throughout their education – at least in an ideal world. But it's not ideal and for children with disabilities a whole different set of additional steps has to be taken. So where to begin to make the whole process mildly less traumatic?

Do your research. Now there's an obvious statement, but you can't possibly have thought I was going to do it for you. If your child has a fairly well-recognised illness then the larger charities and support groups should be able to give you a lot of information on this area. For the less recognised and rarer conditions I would suggest you begin by requesting the hospital your child attends to organise a full assessment incorporating developmental, fine motor and gross motor skills as well as psychological aspects of their wellbeing. I found this an excellent starting point for establishing the help my child might need, and it could also, at a later date, be used as good ammunition in our fight for funding.

Then get hold of a beginner's guide to the statementing process – which involves getting your local authority to recognise your child's needs and cater for them – and try to get your head around that. If ever a day comes when parents aren't totally exhausted by bedtime this topic could certainly be marketed as a great cure for insomnia.

> 'Once we had found the right school for Johnny we sat and planned our tactics. We began by listing all the features the school had, the standard ones and the unique ones too. Then list the fees and costs. Don't kid yourself the

fees are where it ends,' this is where the fight for funding begins. You'll also need to consider transport costs to and from school for example. Finally take your list and mesh it as strongly as possible to your child's needs and condition. We made it clear to the funding authorities that our choice was clearly the only school in the whole country that was right for Johnny. It may be cunning but, after all, the majority of parenting comes down to guerrilla warfare tactics.'

Getting the most out of life

So while on the subject of being cunning, tactical and necessarily manipulative, in the best possible way of course, it's worth looking at other ways in which you will need to develop these skills and how to work the system to get everything you both need and are entitled to.

Many charities exist that Joe Public remains completely unaware of, which have been established to provide funding for a whole range of needs from a holiday to a new carpet. Find out about them through your local Social Security office, who have access to these particular resources, and by pestering the Children and Families or Special Needs teams. I presented our social workers with a comprehensive list of my son's needs and let them take care of the rest. After all, it's what they're paid for. It's worth moving away from the stigma attached to the very title 'social worker' and its link to the parenting police. Swallow your pride: believe me, every little helps.

The government also has a little-known scheme called

the Family Fund that receives very minimal media attention. So most people haven't even heard of it. Not surprising really when you consider it is a government body distributing the money. They supply a whole range of things to people with children who have special needs. From money for leisure outings and holidays to a new washing machine and tumble drier: we got them all. I thank them on a daily basis as I walk around my kitchen and peruse my array of white goods. Apply and take as much pressure off yourself as possible.

Even if you don't need to make such applications it is still well worth while getting a Special Needs social worker on your side. Show them you are not a moaner, or a pain in the proverbial backside, and get them firmly on the team. There will doubtless come a time further down the line when their support will prove invaluable. And, just like the medics, if they feel appreciated they'll work a lot harder for you, finding all those hidden extras that aren't common knowledge out there in the public arena. Take my word for it. In my now dim and distant former life before parenthood hit me, social work was my nine-to-five routine and there was rarely anything more satisfying than finding resources for people who needed them and genuinely appreciated your help. It made local government work worth while!

Sticks and stones . . .

'Sticks and stones may break my bones but words can never hurt me.' Just let me near the smug bastard who is responsible for that particular throwaway comment and I'll give him a dressing-down that would reduce the toughest of the tough to tears. He was obviously a resilient individual because frankly, in my albeit limited experience, words, particularly when spoken in relation to your child, have the capacity to be excruciatingly painful. Unfortunately, insensitive and ill-considered comments are, however unintentional, often a daily part of life.

> 'You find that people talk to your child as though he is thick so often that you either develop an imperviously thick skin or, as we did, learned ways of showing people, however subtly, that Johnny is far from stupid. Just that little bit of discomfort and embarrassment soon teaches them not to treat him differently and not to speak about him in a patronising manner when he is around. Nor, for that matter, when he's not. I'm staggered by how often people will repeat things twice to Johnny, talking to him as though he has no understanding, or worse still they raise their voices as though he were deaf. And, to add insult to injury, they regularly adopt the most bizarre tones of voice when speaking to him. He's fifteen not a baby, or, worse still, a pet. Yes, we get hurt sometimes, but then so does everyone – that's part of life, we're not unique in that. You just have to find ways to overcome these inevitable situations. Just look at your child and imagine how he is feeling.'

Unfortunately, a recent excursion with my son has not yet receded to become a dim and distant memory, although I live in hope. My toddler and I were browsing the bread options in the local supermarket when his illness 'kicked in' as it is prone to do, particularly in public places and generally at full volume. Out of nowhere he hit what can only best be described as a 'middle-aged posh lady' over the head with a packet of croissants as she bent down to retrieve her chosen loaf. I sometimes wish I could wear a label stating that he has a rare brain condition that can result in these embarrassing moments, but somehow that doesn't quite seem reasonable.

So instead of whipping out the home-made explanatory badge, the best option appeared to be to try to deal with him while simultaneously apologising to her. It was only when she grabbed his arm in a vice-like grip to admonish him, before announcing in no uncertain terms that I represented all that was wrong with parents these days, that I completely lost the urge to apologise, or even explain. I just felt the overwhelming desire to follow in my son's footsteps, only this time perhaps with canned produce.

I can only conclude that sometimes walking away is the best and safest option for all concerned.

In my experience, and that of others faced with similar situations, being open with your child about his difficulties and the possible knock-on effects can help enormously. But it's worth bearing in mind that tackling this subject in an age-appropriate manner is probably the most effective way to achieve the results you want. Explaining to my six-year-old child that he has pseudotumourcerebri as well as hypogammaglobulinaemia is never quite going to do it for him. It's also worth bearing in mind that this probably isn't a one-shot explanation type of scenario. As my son develops so does the level of understanding he requires.

I know I am certainly far from out of the woods after our recent and first conversation on this one.

However hard I may try to take life one day at a time, often several days or even decades can attack me at once. So when other people ask what's wrong I often just smile sweetly at the inquisitive party and ask them 'Why?' which usually puts paid to further unwanted investigations. Alternatively, on days when I feel mildly less overwhelmed by life, I've opted to say my son is 'having a few health problems but doing well and heading in the right direction, thank you', despite the fact that he is officially registered disabled.

Labelled for life is a career move I am trying to avoid for my son, but it is nigh on impossible even in today's so-called enlightened world to deny that stigma does unfortunately exist around certain illnesses. So making positive statements in response to negative misconceptions can help enormously and is probably a step in the right general direction.

On the plus side . . .

In spite of all the difficulties and heartbreak that go hand in hand with having a child with special needs, whatever the degree, there's much good to be found in it.

> Johnny's mother concludes that it has shaken up her own values and that her faith in human nature has been restored by 'meeting a nicer class of young people, from those who work fulltime in his current school to those who come to help in the school holidays to my daughter's friends'. She describes them as 'far more giving than I

> remember being at that age. Johnny's condition wasn't forced upon them, they have chosen it as a way of life and are somehow capable of displaying tireless devotion, and it is a privilege to spend time in their company.'

As for faith, many parents I've come across have described it as being a source of great comfort. To others it remains a mystery. Despite the relentless inevitability of health scares and crises an unwell child brings, having him has also provided me with many opportunities to discuss this topic with others in similar situations. And I've reached a stage now where I can live more comfortably with human frailty. I tend to come down on the side of believing that we get what we get in life, and ultimately any true and lasting value lies in how we deal with it. Someone once offered me a great quote during one of our crises and I hang on to it on a daily basis: 'Turn your face towards the light, even when you do not see.' Sometimes I may not even be sure what, and in which direction, the light is, but it does, at least, keep me facing in the right way.

The final word? The power of a parent's ability to multitask should never be underestimated and the parents of special needs children are undoubtedly entitled to wear red pants on the outside of their trousers and sport rather attractive blue capes with 'S' emblazoned across the back. However, don't forget the moments when you need to cast off the cape, put your feet up with a cup of something strong and resume real life a little later. After all, life will still be there when we get back.

With thanks, appreciation and admiration to Johnny and his family.

Wipe wisdom

- Try to ensure you have good friendships around you and find other people with similar difficulties; emotional support, shared experience and goals really do help.
- Accept all the professional support you need, and consider counselling if you feel it would help.
- Work towards acceptance of the situation and peace of mind; it is possible.
- Breaks make all the difference; you're still allowed some pleasure out of life.
- And for when the going gets tough find a reason for living – and what better reason than your child.
- Don't lose heart.

14

Repetitive Strain . . .

Do you honestly want another?

More children? I don't think so. Quite tired enough already, thanks. But that's a personal choice and one made from practical considerations too.

The first to arrive has turned your life upside down, quite literally. Why have more? Particularly as the once normal 2.4 nuclear family is less than the norm today. Is it because you're the natural earth-mother type? Do you crave big hips and days filled with casseroles and finger painting? Perhaps your partner harbours a secret desire for an MPV, and one bursting at the seams at that? Or is it merely because it's expected of us, or simply unwise to have an only child? What's it really like to stop at one or take that leap of faith from one to two, from two to three, and from three to even more? How do we negotiate the changes to our lives, their lives and meet everyone's needs in the process? How big an age gap should we leave? What if they're all boys and you secretly craved a little girl? How do we deal with sibling rivalry and help them become friends while we stay sane? How do we let each child be as individual as they are and have the right to be? And more importantly, will there ever be any time for you and your partner again?

Just one

Who wants to be responsible for rearing another proverbially spoiled child? I will, thanks, if it's all the same to you. Despite the proverb I'll be sticking at one for now because, OOPS, no fat gold band glinting on my finger so probably best to run the risk of raising a little monster, and save my energies for damage limitation. Strangely, I'd prefer to be married and somewhat more secure next time before embarking along that one-way street again. But hey, each to their own. There's no denying that parenthood is the best thing that ever happened to me, but single parenthood? In my experience it's not all it's cracked up to be. And that wasn't much to begin with. So these days when, faced with someone else's newborn bundle of joy, my biological clock forgets that I already have one alarm bell alive and ringing, I simply wind the tape forward to remove all urges successfully. But perhaps I'm alone in feeling that way. Perhaps there are one hundred and one other reasons why couples have only one child. And if so, I want to know about them, not least to back up my own decision to stick at one when the hormones raise hell.

> 'I've never been absolutely clear as to why we only had one child, and in many ways realising that makes me slightly uncomfortable. I suspect that it was really my husband's decision, although we've never talked about it. This is his

second marriage and I know that he dearly wanted to have a child with me but he already had another one with his first wife and consequently I don't think he minded so much if we didn't have any more. I suspect the reason is also partly financial. When we had our son we were in dire financial straits with a property in negative equity amongst other nightmares. There was this unspoken assumption that we could be a working couple with one child but having a second would make it all a little too difficult to balance. Having already got a child he was far more aware than I was of just how much they change your life and quite how demanding they are, physically, emotionally, financially . . . Although I would have liked another and still would some days, I think we were right to stop at one. It would probably have just been too much pressure on our relationship and life in general.

'The plus side of having just one is immense. It allows me to concentrate on all his needs and results in enormous pleasure alongside the inevitable pain! He's really, really special to us which I know two or more would all have been, but with just one I haven't had to divide my time and attention in the same way. Having been one of four girls I also have vivid memories of the sibling rivalry which I struggled with and found quite painful. Also I remember how often my mother couldn't buy something for one of us, or send one of us on a longed-for school trip, because that would have meant doing it for all four and the expense would have become unbearable. So we sacrificed a great deal in many ways, while having just one has meant we can afford a great deal more for him and hopefully provide him with more choices as he grows up.

'The worst aspect has to be his inability to entertain himself. As a baby he got all my attention and that never changed. I was so smitten with him, but never having to cater for another one has resulted in a child who expects a lot of attention. I never get a minute's peace and now he is getting older, when his friends come to play I realise just how much I have worn myself out. Holidays are also difficult as we never get a moment alone and he has no other children around to play with, so we have to choose our destinations carefully.

'The other thing I struggle with is my perception of how other families see us. I feel as though we're sometimes not perceived as a complete family. Whether that's a hangover from the days of the 2.4 nuclear family or just because most of my friends have more than one, I don't know, but I'm acutely aware of feeling "less than" from time to time. It's almost as though when I have a rant about how hard being a mum is I imagine they are all saying, "You've only got one, what would you know?" The truth is though that I do know. I know having more than one child must be extremely hard. I also know that only having one is just as difficult, in different ways.'

Sarah, thirty-nine, mother of Joseph, seven

'We were only just married and thinking about a child when oops, there we were – imminent parenthood looming on the horizon. As for a second or third, I think we might stop at one, not least because right now I feel as though I've just gone through the equivalent of the Vietnam War. The first four or five months were like a never-ending assault course and I want some time to be me again. If we have another one later – great. But I was over forty for the first and the wait might just mean it's too late.

'The truth is that I say I'm happy to stop at one but whilst there is only a slim chance of us having more, in reality I worry about her being an only child. We're admittedly extremely lucky to have her at all and she is, without a doubt, the most precious person in my life. But whilst her standards of living, and ours, might well be better as an only one, the truth of the matter is that I fear "Only Child Syndrome". The fact that they have such a reputation for being selfish and self-centred draws me to wanting a second. I worry, also, that she will have to carry burdens from us, our every aspiration will be placed firmly on her. To be the eldest is tough enough. To be the only one, I fear, may be tougher. As it is, her father already wants her to be Prime Minister. No pressure there then! Thinking about it – roll on the second.'

Joyce, forty-four, mother of Niamh, two

Double the trouble

So times two, or more than double? I have my suspicions it's the latter. But how you begin to prepare your first child for the new arrival and yourself for another dose of childbirth I can't begin to imagine. How do you involve your first child with the baby's care, while also finding time for each child alone, never mind your partner. And that's before you develop the skills necessary to work in the diplomatic corps and act as arbitrator between your growing and warring offspring, who despite an underlying fierce tribal loyalty are guaranteed to bicker on a more than regular basis. From one to two. Not a clue. Never been there and perhaps I never will. But while I groan under the strain of successfully managing one I confess to feeling sometimes more is the pity. Biological urges aside I know that when my son has friends to play, or sleepover, that they entertain themselves with almost complete success, leaving me more time to myself and the one hundred and one neglected chores of the past six years. But is that a good enough reason to have another? Are the financial pitfalls alone simply too terrifying?

'Our first child was purely nature's decision, whilst the second was definitely planned – by me, though my husband didn't protest too much. Also, it happened so quickly that he didn't have a great deal of time to think about it either! The financial cost of two really wasn't an issue when we decided to have our second. Not because we're really rich, more because whilst it is at least twice the work it isn't twice the cost. An extra mouth to feed doesn't double the shopping bill. My daughter doesn't double any of the other household bills either. So that wasn't an issue. Space was a far greater problem but that got resolved by moving! My other main concern I suppose was the childcare aspect of two. Particularly because I work and I was concerned that whilst I had good cover for my son the logistics of organising it for two might prove impossible.

'The best aspect of having two is that I love them both so much and wouldn't be without them. Also, as an added bonus I have one of each, so I get to play football with my son and dress my little girl in a lot of pink and flowery things too!

'The downside is that I no longer have a life. What used to be mine now revolves entirely around them, and will do until they're eighteen so I'm told! Our sex life is non-existent now. That's a blessing! I'm too tired so now it's reserved for high days and holidays, birthdays and Christmas. Isn't it great! Truthfully, though, my husband is jealous of the children in many ways. Not just the effect on our relationship but even down to little things like my buying all the children's clothes for them whilst I expect him to fend for himself in that department. Fair enough, I'd say, but I think he'd tell you otherwise. Fundamentally it's an issue rooted in the children now getting all of my attention, whereas it used to be devoted to him.

'The hardest thing for me about two children is the sibling rivalry. It's a big, big issue in our house. My son loves his sister but can't stop picking on her. Whenever I give any attention to her he reacts and after a while it takes its toll.

'Looking back over the last couple of years I realise that no one can ever prepare you for having children. But when they come, that's it. Small humans control your life from then on. If I'm honest, whilst I wouldn't be without them today, if I could have my time again I wouldn't have had children at all. I love them to bits and would hate anything to happen to them but today my life is no longer my own and I would have had the opportunity then to be selfish, pursuing my career which I love, travelling, and on, and on . . .'

Sheila, thirty-eight, mother of Sam, eight, and Susie, five

'The number one kid in our house – the prototype – is Daisy, now aged three and a quarter. The number two is Jack, seven months. What's it like going from one to two? It's more than double the trouble. You think, Hey, you've already done one, you know the ropes, everything's in place, surely it's like riding a bike, once you've done it, it becomes easy.

'It does NOT. At least it doesn't when your first child is only just out of nappies herself.

'In a two-parent set-up, the great plus point of having just the one offspring is that you outnumber it by two to one. By having two, you chuck away your numerical advantage. And it's then the chickens come home to roost. Suddenly there's no slack time. No R and R. If you're not wiping number one's bottom, you're wiping number two's bottom. There's no time to slope off to the pub. No time to make a cup of tea and read the paper. No time even to go to the loo uninterrupted. The pressure becomes more or less constant.

'As for sleep, you can more or less forget it. Some parents sleep-train their children. This is something we never managed. The result has been nocturnal pandemonium. Jack refuses to fall asleep without bodily contact. If he doesn't GET bodily contact, well, he just might as well scream the house down. Daisy wakes up in the middle of the night and decides having a bed all to herself is not to her taste, particularly when it sounds like party time in the room next door. Much better somehow to infiltrate some more intricate sleeping arrangements and make up a foursome.

'The night is an expedition to purgatory. Fingers in eyes. Knees in groins. Arms bereft of circulation. And the occasional thud and groan of fallen bodies.

'The "advantages" of having two? You don't have to buy

a whole lot of babygros, and you've still got the Moses basket, cot, highchair, soft toys etc. from last time. You're also a damn sight more casual in your approach. If you lavished the same care and attention on number two as you did on number one you'd go round the bend. Anyway, number one won't let you.

'And finally, the plus side of all this – and there HAS to be a plus side – is that Daisy loves Jack to bits. And although Jack hasn't let on yet, by the way he grins when she comes into his eye line, I'd guess he feels the same way too. I'm sure we'll have to develop the skills of a boxing referee in years to come, once the inter-sibling turf wars start. But for the meantime at least while having two is more than twice the headache of one, it's also much more than twice the fun. Having said that though, two really is the limit.'

With grateful thanks to Mark Whitaker. Reproduced from WIPE *magazine*

Duet, trio, whole damn chorus

Personally I think that if I craved that many children I'd simply opt for a job in a children's home and cut out the painful middleman of childbirth. But despite my own misgivings I am willing to admit that I do envy those friends with vast numbers of offspring, even if only on my son's behalf. They are without a doubt braver parents than me, and, despite their obvious stresses and strains, their children appear to thrive on a life of constant sibling company.

Regardless of the upsides, I doubt this is a scenario I shall ever have to negotiate because by the time I meet someone suitable, frankly I'll be cutting it fine to have another, much less a third or fourth. But perhaps that's a blessing in disguise. It must be a logistical nightmare. It was only last week that a friend accidentally included my son in the school-run head-count and left with entirely the wrong children. I'm not sure my mathematical, or any other, skills are up to the job. Can these brave, multiple-breeding parents ever hope or expect to see themselves, or each other, again?

> 'I had my first child because I was married and had a baby – as you do! I did it right! The second one was an attempt to make my relationship right – and it didn't work. In fact shortly afterwards we separated and I had my third child a few years later with my new partner, who wanted a child probably more than I did at that stage. So whilst my third was planned, I think I did it more for him than for me. The best things about having three children? Flipping heck, there aren't any. They do play together, I suppose, so I do get a degree of free time which I get to use clearing up all the mess they've made, cooking for them and doing their washing . . .
>
> 'The worst aspects? It's hard work! Washing, ironing, sorting out the endless garments, sorting out the headache of childcare for that many and getting any free time for just us, or just me.
>
> 'The eldest boy is probably the most troublesome, I suspect because he was spoiled as the firstborn and always got away with things which means he still tries it on now. Only now it doesn't work so well for him!
>
> 'The effect on my relationship has been enormous too.

I'm always exhausted and never want to have sex these days. We don't have any free time to spend as a couple, or very little anyway. You just can't get rid of three kids. The only time is when they're at school but then we're at work so that we can afford to bring them up.

'To be honest, I really do love them all, and I truly believe I love them all equally despite their totally different characters and behaviour, but if I could have my time again I would probably have stopped at just the two, and perhaps just the one relationship.'

Marie, thirty-nine, mother of Jake, eleven, Joel, ten, and Tania, five

'We didn't mean to have the first child so finding myself with three now is an immense shock when I stop and think about it. When I married my wife a doctor had told her that she couldn't have children so we carried on without contraception and it was a great surprise and joy in our first year married when she became pregnant. When number two arrived eighteen months later the fact that she had been told she couldn't conceive was a rather lame excuse! We had been relying on the rhythm method, so it was obviously all down to my timing rather than the time of the month with this one.

'Our third child was a complete mistake and really pissed me off. It had been the usual form of contraception but we were both a lot more careful and I think we were both very shocked when we found out the news. With two we had been perfect and nuclear somehow. With three, God knows what we'd be like. Before we got the news there was some light at the end of the tunnel of having small babies, then suddenly there was at least another two years of hell to come. The absolute killer for me was finding out that the third was on the way and realising that the totally cool solution to my life and a family of two was going to have to be sold. My vintage Porsche with us in the front and two small nippers in the back was never going to manage three wedged in there. So it had to go. I definitely had a bad case of ante- and postnatal depression.

'Now we're in this situation, permanently, there are a lot of upsides. The best thing is that they outnumber us and there's always a great sense of energy about the place, but the worst aspect is that we are both stressed and overstretched. I find I can feel guilty that I am neglecting them even though I'm here with them a lot. It's almost as though there are so many of them that I can never find enough energy or time to go around and hence the feeling that I'm failing them in some way.

'The third child has to be the easiest. Probably because we were so much more relaxed about babies in general by the time he arrived. It's the middle one who is probably the most complicated and requires the most time and in a way it is the hardest to give that time to him.

'As for our relationship, it's meant there is no time for us. Such a large proportion of our time is spent considering the requirements of the children rather than our personal ones and we've found that if we're not careful that can lead to big problems. Today, having successfully negotiated it, we do try to take some time out just for us to ensure that something still binds us together other than being parents of our brood.'

Daniel, thirty-five, father of Hannah, seven, Kieran, five, and Kester, two

'If anyone ever tells you that breast-feeding is an effective form of contraception don't believe them because that was how we ended up with three. We have three children, all boys and under the age of four. We must be clinically insane. Thankfully as the eldest one is just reaching five and the youngest almost a toddler it does feel as though we are beginning to emerge from the chaos a little. It's been very hard having three that close together but it has meant that we'll get the baby bit out of the way more quickly and haven't prolonged the agony too much.

'With the first I tried so hard to be perfect, to get everything right, and with the second I tried even harder. The greatest thing about three is that now I've let go. I'm so much more relaxed that, as a result, the third is a far easier, more relaxed little baby. None the less, the more there are, the less time there is for each of them individually and the guiltier I feel. I know all the things the books tell me about making sure you have time alone with each, making sure they have clearly labelled toys so they have a sense of ownership, making sure they have space to play away from others. But in reality we'd need a bigger house and one hell of a lot more hours in the day than there are to come close to achieving this. These days I seem to manage them more like a pack of dogs in order to keep a vague semblance of control over the whole situation and for now that works just fine!

'The most infuriating thing is the bickering and rivalry that goes on. Whilst I know they love each other and that these fights are in some bizarre way educational, it drives me to distraction. But there's not a lot I can do about it, so unless someone's about to die or suffer horrific injuries I generally try to let them work it out for themselves which inevitably, or rather eventually, seems to happen. It's at times like these, or when they're being desperately protective of each other, that, when my husband is out at work, it can feel strangely isolating being the only adult in amongst all this chaos!

'The truth is that it's overwhelming sometimes having three children but I don't have to do three times as much – not all the time anyway. Also I have had to learn to accept that things will never be perfect again, not even for a moment, and learn to prioritise and let some things fall off the bottom of the list. I have to be realistic these days or I'd go under. In reality it's very hard to achieve and I have to be quite disciplined with myself, but there really is only so much I can do.

'The other thing that I struggle with from time to time is the belief I always held that I would love them all the same, all the time. The truth? The truth is that I don't. I do love them all of the time but equally and fairly, it's just not always possible.

'Three children . . . I wouldn't have done it differently if I had my time again, but, God, it's hard, and one hell of a steep learning curve, one that doesn't let up for a minute. The rules keep changing on an alarmingly regular basis. It's hard to keep up.'

Sandie, thirty-three, mother of Jamie, four, Mark, three, and Harry, one

Wipe wisdom

From a mother of three:

- Forget the immaculately tidy house, keeping up to

date with all the laundry, the paperwork, and the practicalities of everyday life – no chance.

- Prioritise and let the non-essentials slip off the bottom of the list from time to time.

- But don't let yourself fall off the bottom of the list. Your children don't want a mother who's clinically insane any more than they want a mother who looks like a bag lady.

- Make time for you and your partner, if there is one. Have fun and keep your relationship alive – you'll get to keep your sanity at the same time.

And from me:

- If you've already done it – I take my hat off to you.

- If you're about to do it – I can only wish you luck.

Wipe . . .

Insincere introductions and corny conclusions. Can't stand them, but none the less am compelled to write the latter. My son has revolutionised my life to such an extent he quite simply warrants one, or the other, at least.

As much as he has turned my life upside down and inside out, has brought all my long-held beliefs into question, alongside every one of my values, has made me face my human frailty and nurture his, he has taught me the real meaning of life.

There's no large house, or gravel drive, no unlimited cash or voluntary job to ease my conscience. I was beginning to think life had let me down, but then I got what I truly needed and never really knew I wanted: my son, his unconditional love and my new-found capacity for it.

I may get parenting wrong from time to time, more often than not I'm thinking on my feet, but he has made me face life on life's terms, head-on and become willing to learn, to adapt and to change, on an almost daily basis.

With all the horrors have come the most uplifting and rich experiences of life. Each day when I think I couldn't possibly love him more I am shocked by the fact that I both can, and do.

For him I am for ever grateful.

Index